THE INCREDIBLE
ROUTER

THE INCREDIBLE
ROUTER

JEREMY BROUN

FOREWORD BY ANDREW VARAH

GUILD OF MASTER CRAFTSMAN PUBLICATIONS

First published 1989 by
Guild of Master Craftsman Publications Ltd,
166 High Street, Lewes,
East Sussex BN7 1XU

Reprinted 1991

© Jeremy Broun 1989

ISBN 0946819 17 3

Designed by Bridgewater Design

Printed and bound in Great Britain by
Grosvenor Press (Portsmouth) Ltd

The photographs for the following figures were supplied
courtesy of the manufacturers:
Figs. 1.12, 1.13, 1.14: **Racal.** *Fig. 2.8:* **Bosch.** *Fig.
2.10:* **Hitachi.** *Figs. 2.12, 2.13:* **Makita.** *Fig. 2.14:*
Ryobi. *Figs. 5.10, 5.11:* **Wolfcraft.** *Figs. 1.3, 1.4, 1.5,
1.11, 3.1, 4.11(c), 5.1, 5.2, 5.3, 5.4, 5.5, 5.6, 5.7(a):*
Trend. All other photography © Jeremy Broun 1989.
Illustrations © Jeremy Broun 1989. Project designs ©
Jeremy Broun 1989.

CONTENTS

ACKNOWLEDGEMENTS

First I would like to thank the editorial staff of GMC Publications Ltd for asking me to write this book (Alan Phillips, Bernard Cooper, John Haywood and Roger Buse). It all came about by accident as 'The Incredible Router' was originally my suggested title for one chapter in a book on contemporary furniture projects which we were discussing at the time!

I would particularly like to thank John Haywood, technical editor, and Elizabeth Inman, editor, both of whose guidance was invaluable during the project.

I am very grateful for the cooperation and help given by Jim Phillips of Trend Machinery & Cutting Tools Ltd; he provided all the necessary cutters and various accessories, and allowed me to 'doctor' his drawings of cutters.

Thanks are due to the various router and accessory manufacturers/suppliers who kindly loaned their machines, including Arthur Taverner of Hitachi (UK) Ltd, who generously loaned virtually the entire range of routers; John Bonnet of Black & Decker/ Elu (I am hoping he won't ask for his Work-mate back!); Wayne Allan of Makita Power Tools; Gerry Baker, Managing Director of Ryobi Power Tools, and Judith Barker, PR officer; Robert Bosch Power Tools, and Jenny Wolfe of MPR Leedex, their PR agents; Stan Robertson of Wolfcraft (Zebra Tool Co.); Keith Bunker (Leigh Dovetail Jig) and Raymon Weston of Kington Langley, who showed me how to use it. And gratitude also to John Mills of Westminster Trading Company for loaning the remarkable Zyliss Clamp.

My thanks go too to Vee and Tiggy of Fotek, Bath, who processed my film and also told me about the F-stop; to Paul Glover, student at Rycotewood College who worked on the first copy carving jig prototype, and fellow woodworker Keith Wright from Bradford-on-Avon who helped it along in the eleventh hour; and to Bath Cycle Centre for supplying the wheels. Last but not least, thanks to Karl Andress of Bath who occasionally looked in and kept my workshop tidy during the hectic three months, and to my friend Dee Levey who provided meals, read the script and generally gave moral support throughout the project and never wants to hear the word 'router' again!

PS Thanks again to Alan Phillips who gave me an impossible four-month deadline to write the book! (It would have taken years otherwise!)

DEDICATION

This book is dedicated to Howard Orme, woodwork master at Abbotsholme School (1962). If anybody could make 'drawing an exploded view of a smoothing plane, then naming all its parts' fun – Howard could, but his one fatal mistake was to give me the workshop keys!

FOREWORD

Jeremy and I attended Shoreditch College together, and having known him for twenty-five years, I am delighted to write a foreword for his book on the major passion in his life, woodworking.

Jeremy is vastly experienced, and not only has he survived by making furniture, he has also achieved a very professional product, conceived and created in the minimum of space with the smallest outlay in equipment.

Unlike those of us who are fortunate enough to occupy reasonable-sized premises, Jeremy has always had to cope with small and cramped spaces, often without access to large woodworking equipment. In spite of this handicap he has produced and exhibited pieces throughout the UK, and abroad, which are of an equal standard to those produced by professionals with considerably greater resources. I now know why! Over the years he has perfected his main power tool, the router, to do work which in my workshop would occupy ten machines and acres of floor space!

His talent for relating to both the professional and the layman will guarantee this book space in our workshops. For example, not only does he admit to making errors, but he then goes on to describe how he solved them, thus making us all feel a little less stupid when we encounter difficulties.

I had no idea quite how versatile the router could be until I read Jeremy's book, and I have been using one professionally ever since they first appeared. His illus-trations are excellent, and I am envious of his ability to design pieces which demand care, are aesthetically pleasing, and are created just for this book.

His emphasis on giving a balanced view of the options for the router is excellent, in that he poses an 'either/or' situation, leaving the reader to be the final arbiter as to which router to buy and, almost more importantly, which attachment, as well as which are the most versatile cutters. As any router owner knows, the cutters are soon worth more than the router!

Having read the book I firmly believe that it will stand for many years to come as the 'router bible'. What impressed me most was that in spite of my being a professional furniture-maker for over twenty years, I learnt something new in every chapter. In many cases Jeremy has used the simple expedient of lateral thinking, and 'turning' a complete bowl without a lathe, but with a clever jig, is a good example of this lateral thought.

At a stroke Jeremy offers advice which would have taken us hours to learn, and solves so many general problems that I feel almost guilty taking his years of experience, and trade secrets, merely for the cost of buying this book.

Andrew Varah
Little Walton
Warwickshire

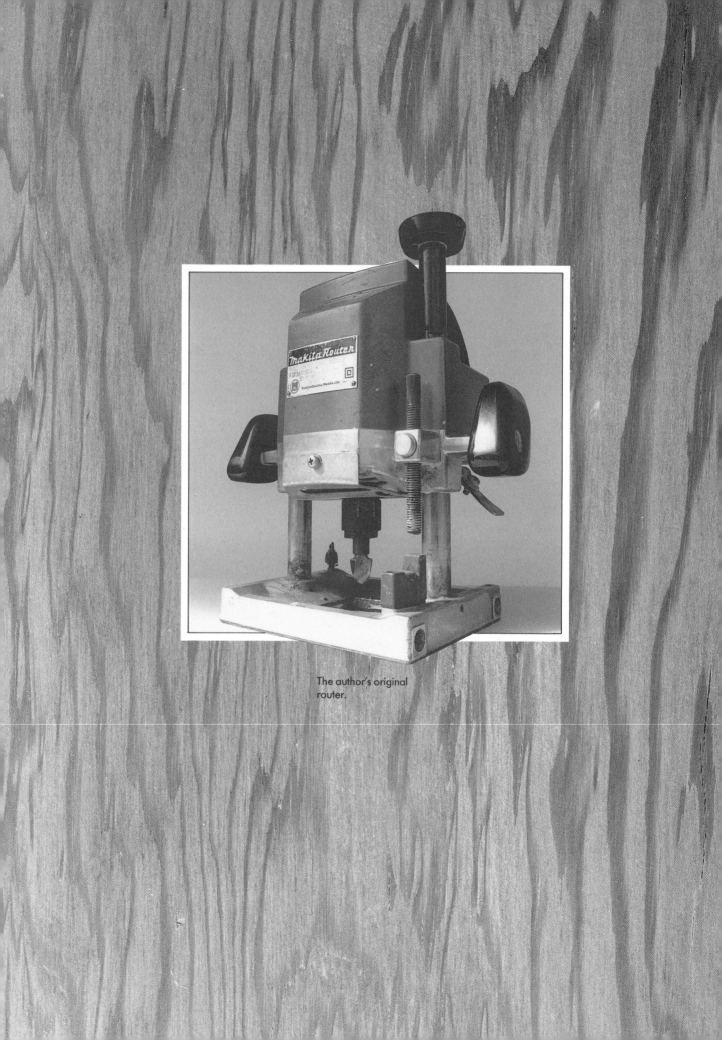

The author's original router.

INTRODUCTION

In 1974 a salesman walked into my workshop and tried to sell me a gadget called a router. I told him he was wasting his time as I could not afford such toys, but he offered to leave it with me for a few days to play with. When he returned we entered into a credit agreement and I would say now that if I could take only one tool to my desert island – it would be that router.

Of course the router is nothing new and has been widely used in the furniture and construction industries for decades, but amateurs and professionals alike are only just beginning to realise its full potential.

I have come to regard the router as being a creative problem solver, and indeed more than that – almost a workshop friend! There is something rather magical about it; this simple concept has virtually revolutionised woodworking. As a 'Jack of all trades', it might seem to run the risk of being 'master of none', but that is not so.

The router is very much the tool of the late twentieth century, for not only can it copy the past but it is beginning to shape the future, making possible new ways of fashioning wood, and earning it the reputation of being very much a tool in its own right. It can do virtually anything!

To do justice to this tool, I have designed a range of projects which I hope will appeal to a wide variety of readers, whether they be young, old, male, female, total beginners or advanced woodworkers. However, this is not just a projects book; it is more an adventure into routing, using a range of techniques delivered through a series of projects which will, I hope, give the reader at *any level of skill* much pleasure to make and live with.

All you need is a router, a workspace, a few extra tools and some enthusiasm to take up my invitation to share some of the creative magic of . . . the incredible router.

HOW TO USE THIS BOOK

Although various general topics have been pigeon-holed into chapters, there is much cross-fertilisation of ideas in the book, and the projects and preliminary chapters are closely related.

For convenience, the projects have been designated a star rating:

★ — Introductory (requiring no previous experience)

★★ — Intermediate (some experience of woodworking)

★★★ — Advanced (up to exhibition standard)

There is something for everyone, and the projects have been presented in an open-ended way which allows room for interpretation. You may wish to start with the easiest and work through, or to pick the ones which particularly appeal, but I hope the book will provide many years of challenging enjoyment, whatever your level of skill.

Fig. 1.16 The router
unpacked for the first time.

1 THE INCREDIBLE ROUTER

What is a router? How does it work? What does it do and how do you use it?

The concept is so simple that it hardly requires an explanation, but before I offer one anyway, let's look at woodworking generally.

Suppose you want to smooth a piece of wood flat, cut a dovetail or perhaps a mortise and tenon joint, cut a wooden screw thread, make a salad bowl, carve a wooden spoon, build a staircase, inlay the edge of a cabinet, or just drill a hole and make some dowel to fit into it – well, the router will do all that, and more. In fact it will tackle just about any task in wood!

It is essentially a **high-speed electric drill** which has a **sharp-edged cutter** (Fig. 1.1) in its chuck instead of a drill bit. This rotates at a very high speed (rpm) and engages in the wood through an opening in the base of the tool. The whole device is usually **hand held** and moved across the wood so that the hole which the cutter has made in the surface is translated into a **groove** (Fig.

High-revving electric motor (8–25,000 rpm)

Motor body is attached to router base by two columns

Handles

Chuck

Spring-loaded plunging action

Precision cutter

Base

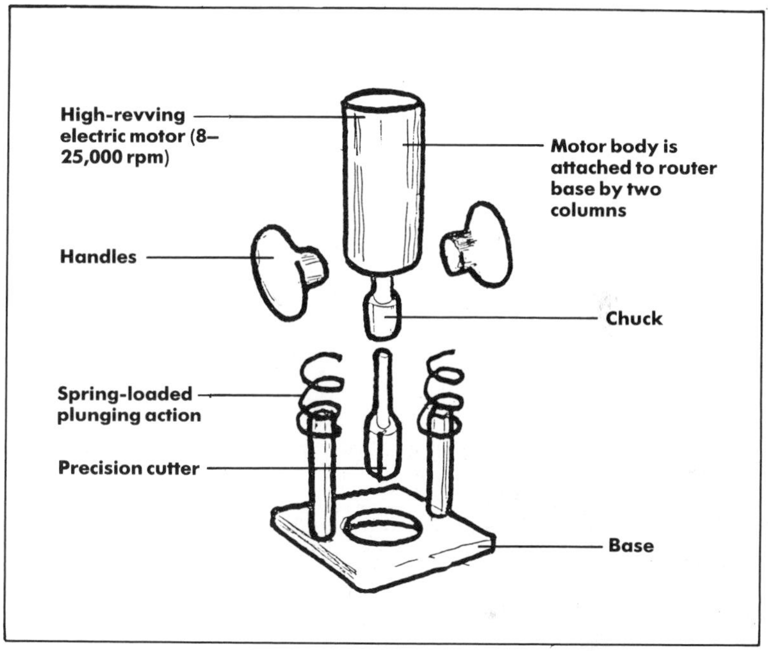

Fig. 1.1. The basic components of the router.

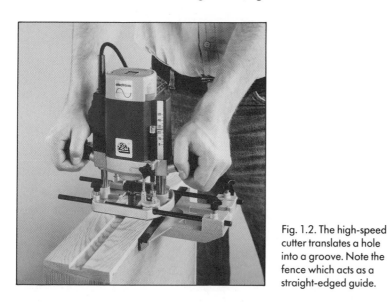

Fig. 1.2. The high-speed cutter translates a hole into a groove. Note the fence which acts as a straight-edged guide.

1.2). I say it is usually hand held, but it can also be **mounted on a table** – either underneath (**inverted routing**, Fig. 1.3) or on top (**overhead routing**, Fig. 1.4).

Routers are either **fixed base** or, more commonly, **plunging.** By attaching various steadying devices such as a **fence** (see Fig. 1.2), the movement of the router can be controlled. A **plunging and locking device** also gives control when the cutter is lowered and raised at the beginning and end of the cut (Fig. 1.5).

To say the router is a grooving tool is merely to hint at its capabilities. Consider the three main factors which give the router its incredible versatility:

1 The power rating (measured in watts from about 400w to 2000w).
2 An infinite variety of cutter profiles producing just about any conceivable shape in wood (Fig. 1.6).

Fig. 1.3. Inverted routing.

3 Jigs and attachments.

These three factors are dealt with in chapters 2, 3 and 5, but just a brief further mention about cutters here.

Cutters range from just under 2mm in diameter to about 30mm or so. They rotate at 20 000–25 000 rpm (although the latest generation of electronic routers operate at between 8000–25 000 rpm) which is a phenomenal speed. The **larger the cutter,** ideally the **slower the speed.** Consider, for example, the bulk of metal at the tip of a smoothing plane and the speed at which it passes over the wood, then consider the rate of feed of a 1.6mm diameter cutter which is smaller than a match-head! (Fig. 1.7.)

It is easy, and common, to expect far too much of this tool and try to take too much wood away too quickly. The result is smoke, burnt wood, overload on the router and the ruination of an expensive cutter.

Fig. 1.4. Overhead routing.

As a general rule, if you cut down into the wood – **depth of cut** – half the diameter of the cutter you won't go far wrong. Obviously where straight cutters are concerned, a specific depth of cut can be routed in stages (Fig. 1.8), and depends on surface contact.

So how is the portable router used? Well, let's first consider safety, since the most important thing in any craft is 'safety first'!

SAFETY

A router is an electric gadget passing a current in the UK of 220–240 volts. Like many readers, no doubt, I have taken the full dose at least once in my life, but for some people that could have *cost* them their life.

On one occasion I was changing an old light switch to a new one. I took the precaution of removing the appropriate fuse from the fuse box, but it was a hot summer's day and my fingers were sweaty. The shock I encountered must have cooked my bones instantly as my fingers ached for days. (I should of course have turned off the master switch.)

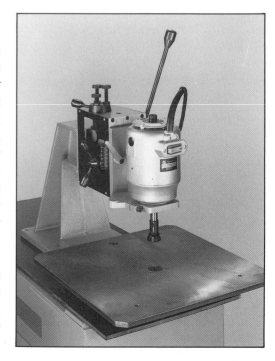

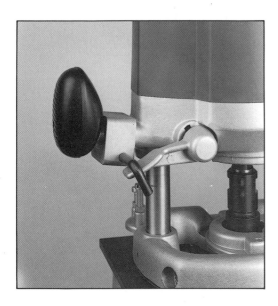

Fig.1.5. The plunging and locking device.

I also recall that a Scandinavian school friend of mine, whom I visited in Norway several times, died in the prime of his youth while changing the fuses during a blackout at a social event. I tell these stories for a good reason.

The router should be correctly wired, ideally in unbreakable plugs, and earthed. It is **quite easy to cut through the cable** by mistake, so a stout router cable to start with is preferable, and constant checks should be made that it is intact.

It should **never** be switched on at the wall while the cutter is being changed because in handling and rotating the router the switch could be knocked on. I try as far as possible to hang the cable **above** me so that I do not trip over it or entangle it, etc.

The advent of plunging routers has dramatically improved their safety, as there is little need for a cutter to protrude until it is about to be fed into the work. The damage a rotating cutter can do to human flesh does not bear contemplating, but you would be surprised how easy it is to gash yourself on a stationary cutter – not just mounted in the router, but when handling it and particularly while setting up.

Because the router removes wood by a rapid rotating action, the wood particles are a mixture of chippings and dust. Both

Fig. 1.6. These six cutters can produce an infinite variety of shapes, and they are just half a dozen out of a thousand.

are hazardous to eyes and ears in particular. Now, I always protect my ears with **earmuffs**. In the early days I paid scant attention to this, and now my hearing is affected.

Eyes are very vulnerable, for the rotating cutter causes fine and not-so-fine particles of dust to fly out in any direction. I have to admit that I feel inhibited wearing **protective glasses** because dust particles get everywhere, including on to the glass. Perhaps the best form of protection offering the maximum visibility is a **visor**.

The other main hazard, of which we are increasingly aware, is dust which is inhaled. Certain hardwoods are known to be toxic, and with the increased use of manufactured boards – plywood, chipboard and MDF (medium density fibreboard) – the risks are greater because of the bonding resins used. Also, in the case of MDF the very fine 'fluff' resulting from machining is dangerous.

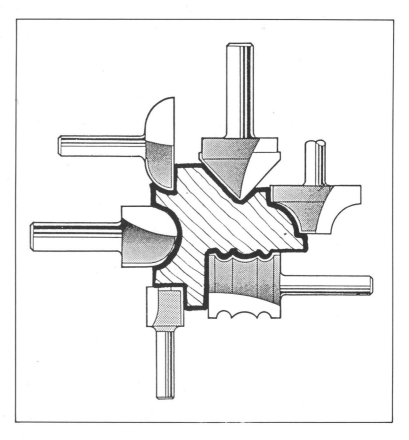

It is important to use a **dust mask** at all times and there are numerous designs on the market. At the end of the day you can check to see how well it is working. A dust film will penetrate down the sides of a badly fitting mask and up around the nostrils. I tend to use the throw-away paper ones with a wire tightening clip which contours round your particular nose! (Fig. 1.9.)

The other way of dealing with dust is to extract it at source by attaching a **dust extraction unit** to the router (Fig. 1.11). Of course if safety were taken to its limits, we would all be dressed like spacemen and not be in contact with the material at all.

Racal Panorama Ltd is a company which supplies a wide range of products, including: a **faceshield**, which is a comfortable, lightweight, fully adjustable head harness and visor ideal for routing (Fig. 1.13).

Earmuffs (Fig. 1.9.) that most essential piece of protective equipment, come in the shape of the Ultramuff 2 for high

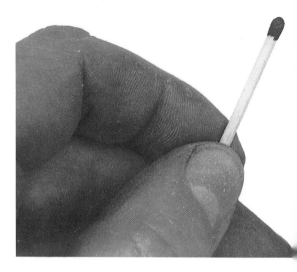

Fig. 1.7. A 1.6mm diameter cutter – smaller than a match-head.

Fig. 1.8. A specific depth of cut can be routed in stages with a straight cutter.

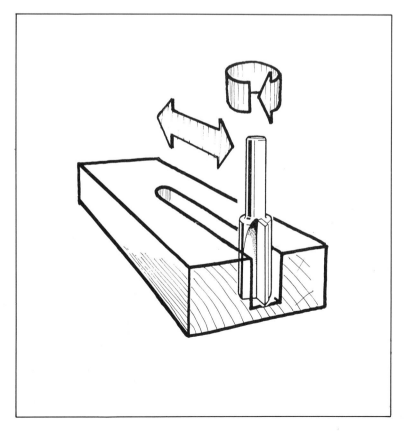

frequency noise attenuation.

The 5060 Dustmask is lightweight, comfortable and effective (Fig. 1.13) and for combined dust and eye protection the Dustmaster Mk2 powered respirator must be the ultimate surely! (Fig. 1.14.)

The final word about safety when routing is, 'Never run in the workshop', as I used to tell my eager young students. Joking apart, don't be in too much of a hurry as this does lead to accidents. The router should be switched off whenever changes are made, always placed on its side with the cutter facing away from you when you put it down, and do as I do – **respect all machines with fear!**

OPERATION

Having considered safety first, we can now look at how to operate the incredible router.

Any manual or 'motor' skill relies on a cycle of activity between the brain and the hands. The central mental activity which commands the hands to 'do a task' is **perception** (the core mental activity of all behaviour), and can simply be described as 'looking for meaning'. In order to perceive, we use the various senses of sight, sound, touch and smell.

Through our eyes, ears, nose, nerve endings and bones, we take in messages.

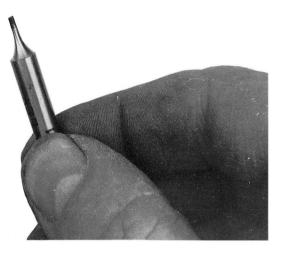

Familiar messages are quickly 'perceived' and the response is automatic and fast, as in riding a bike or tying up shoelaces. Learning any new skill is a process of perceiving unfamiliar messages, and the response is slow, uncertain, clumsy and 'unskilled'. Fig. 1.15 – a model I designed many years ago – illustrates this.

In routing we receive messages through our senses of touch, sight, hearing and, indeed, smell as to how the tool is performing, and I think it is useful to understand a little about the process when trying to master the tool.

So, having broadened our horizons a little about the nature of hand work or manual skill, we can now deal with mastering the skill of routing.

After taking your new router out of its carton (Fig. 1.16, see page 10) and reading the handbook to see how the accessories fit on, etc., the first thing to do is **fit a cutter** into the **collet** with the **spanners** provided. There is a knack to this, as it is all too easy when tightening, or especially loosening, a cutter, for the spanners to slip and for you to graze your fingers against the router. I tend to line up the spanners for each operation and use my **hand as a vice** (Fig. 1.17) which is more powerful and controllable than using two hands.

After many years of routing, I still get confused about which way the spanners should turn to loosen/tighten the cutter. It is easy to get disorientated if the router is not

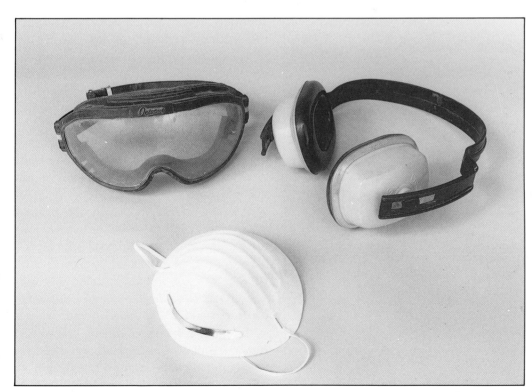

Fig. 1.10. The ultimate in protective clothing.

Fig. 1.9. Protective glasses, earmuffs and dust mask.

facing the same way each time you change cutters (rather like trying to work out which way the clock hands rotate when looking at the clock while standing on your head). To tighten the cutter, however, you always use the spanners in a clockwise direction.

The cutter should be inserted **all the way home,** then **withdrawn fractionally.** This apparently avoids longitudinal vibration which could cause it to work loose, but it should not be over-tightened. I often also use **fibre collet sleeves** which probably take up some of the vibration (available from Method Tools Ltd of Disley).

After selecting a suitable piece of wood and mounting it in the vice or on the bench with G-clamps, you fit the **straight guide fence** on to the router and get ready to start your first routing operation.

You may find the fence fouls the vice or bench, and this raises the whole topic of **holding devices** which is discussed in Chapter 4. The easiest initial exercise is to use a block of wood thick enough to be secured in the vice and allow the fence free access against the edge of the wood.

If you regard the router as a marking gauge which has at its point a cutter which behaves something like a conker being spun on a piece of string at 300 times per second, you have the basic action.

First, check everything is tightened, then start up the router. You will get a **kick,** unless you use an electronic model which has a slow start up. Firmly held in both hands, the router feels something like a giroscope, wanting to **wander** in all directions.

To rout a groove, slide the fence out a little and tighten it, then with the machine switched off practise moving the router along the intended path of the groove with the fence held firmly against the edge of the wood (like a marking gauge). Next, practise plunging the cutter down to the wood, locking, raising it again (it's easy). Now switch on the power and repeat the action, feeding the cutter gently into the wood about two or three millimetres. If the cutter wanders, it is because the fence is wandering, so you should be concentrating on the action of the fence even if you are looking at the cutter! (Fig. 1.18.)

Try taking the fence off and routing a straight groove freehand, and you will soon get the feel of the animal (see Table Mats, page 70).

The great thing about routing is that it is rather like playing squash. This is a game you can play almost immediately and it takes perhaps less skill than tennis to get a

Fig. 1.11. Extracting dust at source.

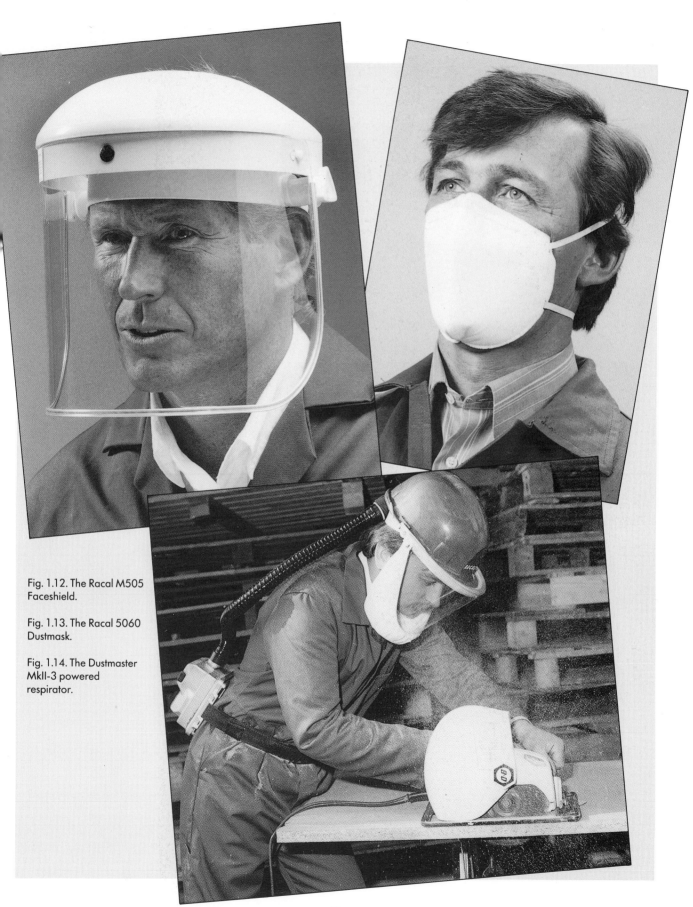

Fig. 1.12. The Racal M505 Faceshield.

Fig. 1.13. The Racal 5060 Dustmask.

Fig. 1.14. The Dustmaster MkII-3 powered respirator.

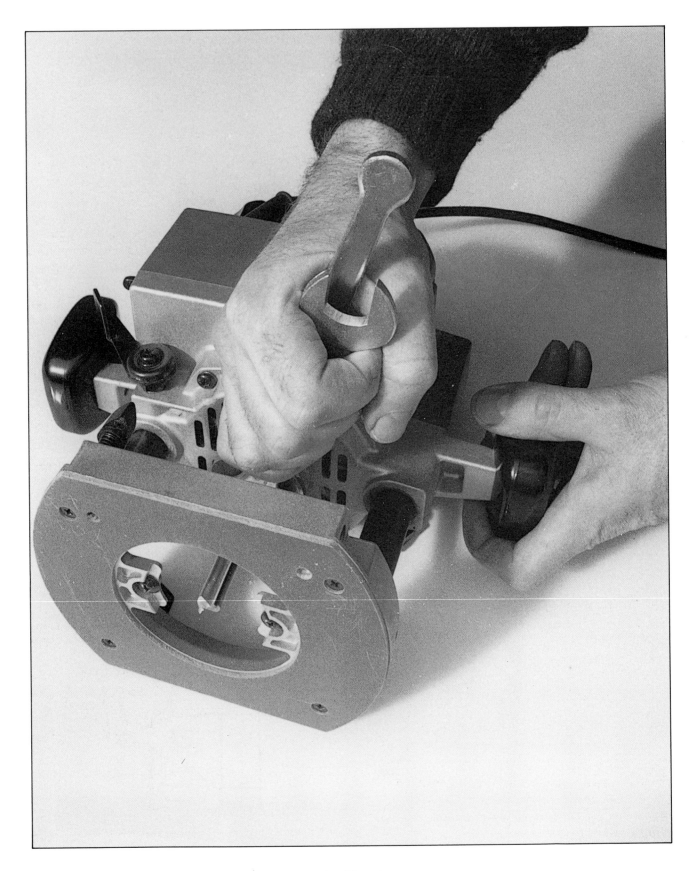

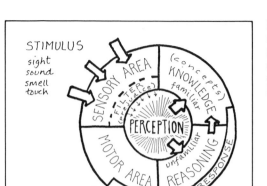

STIMULUS
sight
sound
smell
touch

RESPONSE
through the limbs

Fig. 1.15. The perpetual nature of motor skill (based on Pavlov's stimulus/response/association theory of learning).

Fig. 1.17. Lining up the spanners and using the hand as a vice when tightening or loosening the collet (opposite).

Fig. 1.18. The router in position ready for use.

satisfying result – you don't need to be a world champion to enjoy it. To play the game really well, of course, demands great skill and usually many years' experience. But the principle is simple.

Like any game, routing has a set of rules. Here are some basic ones:

- Ensure the router is the appropriate size/ power rating for your intended tasks and that it is in proper working order.
- Select a suitable cutter for the task and make sure it is in prime condition (razor-sharp and not damaged).
- Check everything is tightened properly on the router, as by virtue of its highly revving motor it is a vibration-prone tool.
- Make a series of light cuts (**passes**) to achieve the desired depth of cut rather than one deep cut.
- Anticipate the action, making a 'dry run' first to check details such as whether the cable is fouling half-way along a pass, or a G-clamp is hindering the fence, or if the router slips at the end of an edge-grooving operation where the end of the board approaches the mouth of the router.
- Maintain the correct **rate of feed** when making a pass – too fast will result in inaccurate work, a broken cutter and overloaded router, while too slow will result in burning.
- Rout into the wood **against** the rotation of the cutter except for cleaning up a cut. It

sometimes helps to rout in both directions to remove burrs.

A router is also rather like a smoothing plane. The cutter (which in the case of a plane is a wide chisel) is held in a jig, and it is the jig which controls the action perfectly. In a plane the blade is not only held at an exact angle in relation to the wood, but the back iron which is attached to the blade fractionally behind its tip ensures the shaving is consistent. Without this the plane would just create a wedge-shaped shaving and get stuck in the wood. We tend to take this sophisticated action for granted, perhaps because the operating controls of a hand plane are so simple. But without the jig the plane blade is merely a chisel, and one of the most difficult woodworking tools to master. Imagine the router cutter just driven by a motor without the router body! The point is that **jigs are essential in routing.**

The router is not only a jig in itself, but relies on jigged attachments to become the incredibly versatile tool it is. Jigs are dealt with in Chapter 6.

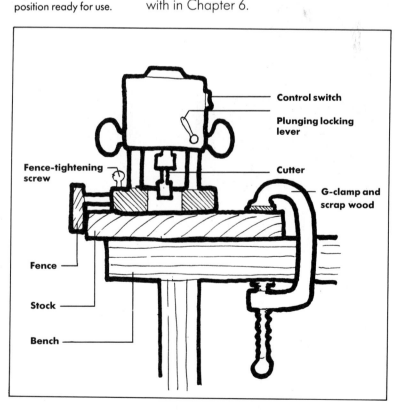

Control switch

Plunging locking lever

Fence-tightening screw

Cutter

G-clamp and scrap wood

Fence

Stock

Bench

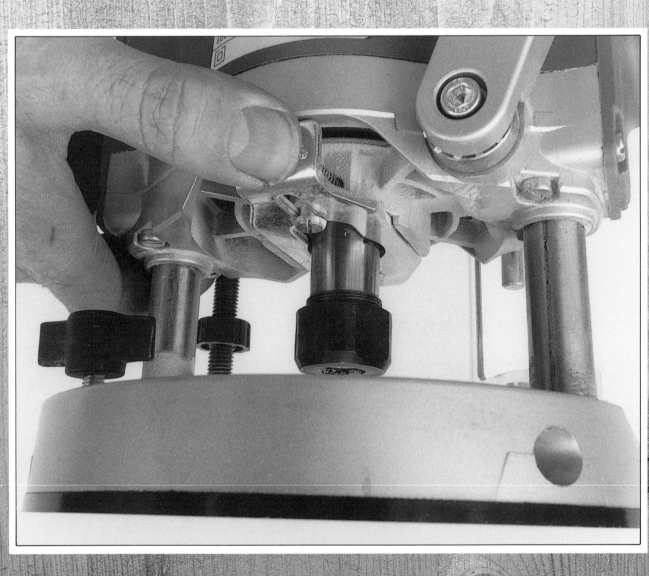

Fig. 2.3. One-spanner
chuck-tightening requires
a spindle-lock.

2 ROUTERS ON THE MARKET

This book has allowed me a unique opportunity to try out a whole range of routers while making the projects. Having used the same router for over fifteen years – my good 'old faithful' Makita 3600B (1500 watts) – which has served me excellently and produced many commissioned and exhibition pieces of furniture, I would probably not otherwise have had the opportunity to get the feel of other routers.

The revolution in plastics and aluminium technology, coupled with microelectronics, has given birth to a whole family of routers of all shapes and sizes, with new models now appearing quite frequently.

I am not offerng a *Which?* report on the current range of routers, as my handling of them has been fairly brief and superficial. Indeed in such a competitive market they all do the job very well and most are excellent value for money. A testament to this is the fact that during the building and photographing of the projects, I attempted to give fair and even exposure to each router on loan. But each time I set up a particular one for a project and started using it, I got 'hooked' and had to remind myself to keep on changing – it is very easy to get attached to a router!

The routers I had on loan were by no means the full range, rather a sampling of the popular models and one or two examples at both ends of the power range.

Of course each router possesses strong and weak points, and it is probably easiest to describe the prerequisites of an imaginary 'ideal' router.

It would include:

■ minimum power rating 750 watts (probably 1500 watts)

■ quiet running
■ comfortable handle grips with low centre of gravity
■ easy access to on/off switch without stretching fingers (a priority)
■ easy access and operation of plunge-lock facility without stretching fingers
■ around 3kg weight
■ easy start up
■ square-sided base (or combination round/square) – for batten routing and so it does not roll off the bench (when the fence is not on)
■ thick electric cable
■ minimum of moving parts (which potentially vibrate loose)
■ good visibility through base
■ easy sub-base connections
■ good plunge facility (60mm plus)
■ dust extraction facility
■ spindle lock for one-spanner chuck-tightening operation
■ rod-type fence arms which can be lengthened
■ simple collet-tightening system (spanner and spindle lock)
■ interchangeable accessories (guide bushes, etc.)
■ simple and easy to operate (with one hand) depth-adjuster and (especially) fine adjuster
■ good spares and service back-up
■ removable base assembly

Obviously, there is not a router on the market which fulfils all those requirements, but the list serves as a guide to the kind of questions you might ask when selecting your own, and if you are going into the business quite seriously (more than just the odd few hours' routing at weekends), then it makes sense to have more than one size of router.

Although for years my workhorse has been the Makita 3600B, I also have a miniature Zinken Gamma 7 (360w) for trimming and shallow housings in cabinets (it stands only 5" high and 'will reach the parts other routers cannot reach'). At the other end of the scale, I have a rather large metal milling machine which I use for wood and plastics (Fig. 2.5).

Concerning power rating, it is really very much a matter of 'horses for courses', and apart from the more limited range of 6mm (¼") shank cutters which the smaller routers (400–750 watts) accommodate, these routers just take longer to do the job because shallower cuts have to be made. Of course the plunge-depth is greater on the larger routers, but I would say a good range of capacity is between 750 and 1500 watts; however, having said that, you can still get

an incredible amount of creative mileage from the smallest routers, as the projects illustrate.

Let's take a look at some of the routers on the market.

First, the typical router is packaged neatly in a box which should include a comprehensive **handbook** giving operating instructions (and some have helpful routing hints), and a kit of **standard accessories** (see Fig. 1.16). These accessories will include a straight guide assembly (fence) and standard 18mm **guide bush,** sometimes a **wheel fence** (or roller attachment, Fig. 2.6) for curved work, a pair of spanners, reducing collets if it is a powerful model, sometimes a straight cutter thrown in, and rarely (one manufacturer only on my sampling) a plug is included – and it's difficult to get your router to work without one!

Incidentally, this manufacturer will supply various optional accessories, such as a range of guide bushes, routing tables,

Fig. 2.4. The 21st-century router!

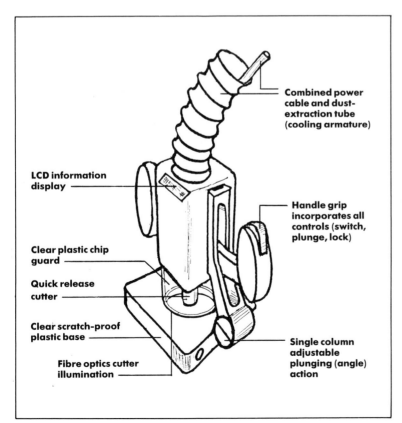

LCD information display

Clear plastic chip guard

Quick release cutter

Clear scratch-proof plastic base

Fibre optics cutter illumination

Combined power cable and dust-extraction tube (cooling armature)

Handle grip incorporates all controls (switch, plunge, lock)

Single column adjustable plunging (angle) action

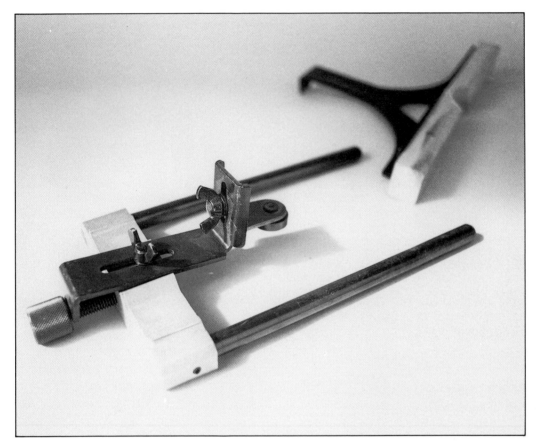

Fig. 2.6. Accessories may include a roller attachment.

Fig 2.5. The author's metal-milling machine (opposite).

dovetailing kits, cutters, etc., and it is best to write to the firm for a catalogue showing the full range.

As this book is predominantly about **creative routing** it is not my intention to explore in depth the technical specifications of routers, which are adequately covered in other publications and by the manufacturers themselves.

I repeat that **creatively** a little can go a long way, and that acquiring the latest gadgetry does not necessarily guarantee creative results. The creativity is largely in the user's head.

Routers on the market:

BOSCH

Robert Bosch Ltd, PO Box 98, Broadwater Park, Denham, Uxbridge UB9 5HJ.
POF 400 (DIY) (400w). Max. plunge 48mm. 6mm collet. 27 000 rpm.
Features. One spanner and spindle lock.

Plastic straight guide assembly. Compact all-in-one plastic moulding design.

POF 500 (DIY) (500w). Max. plunge 52mm. 6mm collet. 27 000 rpm.
Features. Detachable 42mm drive motor. Numerous small accessories included as standard supply.

1601 (Professional) (790w). 6mm collet. 25 500 rpm.
Features. Fixed base.

1603 (Professional) (100w). 6mm/12mm collet. 25 000 rpm.
Features. Fixed base.

1604 (Professional) (1150w). 6mm collet. 25 000 rpm.
Features. Fixed base.

GOF 1600 (Heavy duty) (1600w). 6mm/12mm collet. 22 000 rpm.
Features. Plunging router; clear plastic chippings guard.

GOF 1700E 'Electronic' (1700w). 6mm/ 12mm collet. 8–22 000 rpm.
Features. Built-in spindle lock. Chip protection Plexiglas.

BLACK & DECKER

Westpoint, The Grove, Slough, Berkshire SL1 1QQ.

BD66 (DIY) (480w). 6mm collet. Plunge 50mm. 26 000 rpm.
Features. Slider start/stop switch.

SR100 (DIY) (600w). 6mm collet. Plunge 50mm. 24 000 rpm.
Features. Slider start/stop switch.

ELU

Black & Decker/Elu

MOF96 (600w). 6mm and 8mm collet. Plunge 50mm. 24 000 rpm.
Features. Extensive range of accessories.

MOF96E 'Electronic' (750w). 6mm and 8mm collet. Max. plunge 50mm. 8000–24 000 rpm.
Features. Double-lock cutter tightening. Full range of accessories.

MOF177 (1600w). 12mm collet. Max. plunge 65mm. 20 000 rpm.
Features. Large range of accessories.

177E 'Electronic' (1850w). 12mm collet. Plunge 65mm. 8000–2000 rpm.
Features. Extensive accessories. Double-lock cutter tightening.

HITACHI

Hitachi Power Tools (UK) Ltd, Precedent Drive, Rooksley, Milton Keynes MK13 8PJ.

FM 8 (DIY) (550w). 6mm collet. Plunge 52mm. 27 000 rpm.
Features. Detachable motor (42mm housing).

TR 8 (730w). 6mm collet. Max. plunge 52mm. 24 000 rpm.
Features. Rocker switch.

TR 12 (1300w). 12mm collet. Plunge 52mm.

Fig. 2.1. The Hitachi M12V.

Fig. 2.2. Easy access to the plunge-lock facility is very important.

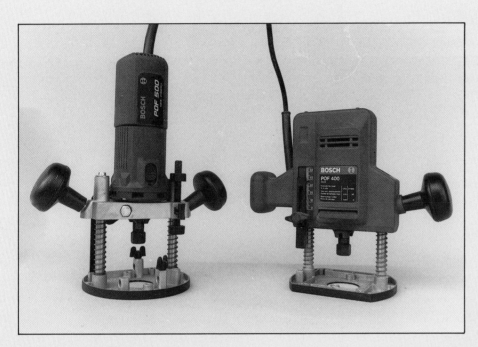

Fig. 2.7 Bosch POF 400 and POF 500.

Fig. 2.9. Bosch GOF 1700E.

8 Bosch GOF 1600.

22 000 rpm.
Features. Circular base.

M 12V 'Electronic' (1850w). 12mm collet. Plunge 62mm. 8000–20 000 rpm.
Features. 18mm guide bush included; spindle lock.

MAKITA

Makita Electric (UK) Ltd, 8 Finway, Dallow Road, Luton, Bedfordshire LU1 1TR.

3700DW (Cordless trimmer) (7.2 volts). 6mm collet. 8000 rpm.
Features. Fixed base; battery powered; 145mm high; various accessories optional.

3601B (930w). 12mm collet. 23 000 rpm.
Features. Fixed base. Generous standard accessories.

3600B (Heavy duty) (1500w). 12mm collet. 60mm plunge. 22 000 rpm.
Features. Oblong base; sprung-screw fine-depth adjuster; straight and wheel guide standard accessory.

3612BR (Extra heavy duty) (1600w). 12mm collet. 65mm plunge. 23 000 rpm.
Features. Various collet sleeves, and accessories.

RYOBI

Luna Tools & Machinery Ltd, 20 Denbigh Hall, Bletchley, Milton Keynes MK3 7QT.

R 150 (750w). 8mm collet. 50mm plunge. 24 000 rpm.
Features. Compact and lightweight; 18mm guide bush template; straight and circular guides.

R 220 (1000w). 12mm collet. 23 000 rpm.
Features. Fixed-base router.

R 500 (1500w). 12mm collet. 60mm plunge. 22 000 rpm.
Features. Compact and powerful; generous accessories.

R 600E 'Electronic' (Heavy duty) (2050w). 12mm collet. 60mm plunge. 10–20 000 rpm.
Features. Externally accessible brushes; see-through protection guard.

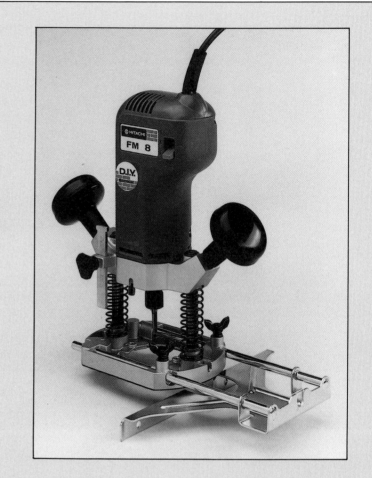

Fig. 2.10. Hitachi FM 8.

Fig. 2.11. (From left to right) Hitachi TR 12, TR 8, FM 8.

Fig. 2.12. Makita 3700 D.

Fig. 2.13.
Makita 3612 BR.

Fig. 2.14. Ryobi R-500.

27

Fig. 3.4. A healthy
collection of cutters

3 CUTTERS

Routing technology has catapulted into significance in recent years with the development of cutters. The incredible router has at the heart of its system the incredible router bit, a razor-sharp and highly precise piece of revolving metal, profiled to cut a thousand shapes (Figs. 3.2(a), (b)).

Cutters are made of **high-speed steel** (HSS) or **tungsten carbide,** usually tipped (TCT). The latter last many times longer, and although more expensive than HSS cutters are more cost-effective. The very smallest cutters (under 3mm diameter) are available in HSS only. The advantage of HSS is that you can grind and sharpen the cutters yourself. The very best cutters (not readily available) are **ceramic** and **diamond,** but obviously they cost many times more than HSS and TCT.

The main sizes of cutter shank diameter are 6mm, 1/4", 3/8", and 1/2", but there are some variations to these sizes amongst router manufacturers. For instance the Makita trimmer I used had a 6mm diameter collet, and as 1/4" = 6.35mm, standard 1/4" cutters would not fit. (This is to limit the size of cutters to prevent the small motor burning out.) 6mm cutters are available from suppliers such as Wolfcraft, who also supply a sleeve for use in 1/4" collets. The important thing is to use the correct collet sleeve for the cutter-shank diameter.

As a general rule, the cutter-shank diameters correspond to the following router power ratings:

1/4" shank: 400w–750w
3/8" shank: 750w–1300w
1/2" shank: 1300w upwards.

The larger routers include shank-reducing collet sleeves for interchanging cutters.

Many cutters come in two shank sizes depending on the diameter of the cutter, and will therefore fit different routers. Obviously, a 12mm diameter cutter will be stronger on a 12mm shank, but then a 6mm shank will only fit the smaller routers.

One of the most satisfying aspects of routing is building up a collection of cutters (Fig. 3.4). They are not cheap, so should be treated with extreme care when handling, using and storing.

Cutters can be re-ground and re-sharpened, although the TCT ones need to be sent away for professional re-shaping.

It is interesting to see how much creative mileage you can get out of just a few well-chosen cutters.

For making the projects in this book, I used the Trend 'Craft Range' of cutters. (More details on Trend and their range of products and services can be found on page 4.) This is a set of 7 popular cutters

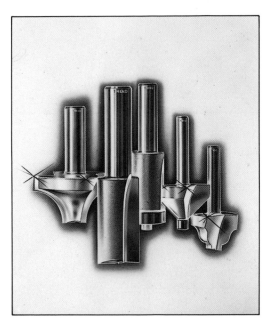

Fig. 3.1. Samples from the range of Trend cutters.

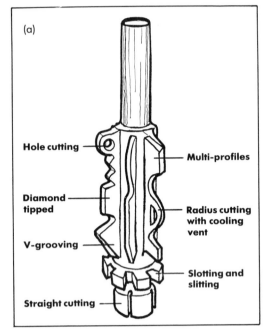

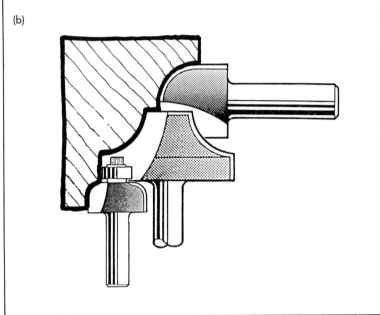

(Fig. 3.5) for such uses as grooving, rebating and engraving. Supplemented by other cutters, it may surprise the reader to learn that only 18 cutters in all were used to make the entire range of projects.

Fig. 3.2 (a). The ultimate fantasy cutter. The JKB universal multi-shape-router-cutter-bit.

Fig. 3.2 (b). Three typical moulded shapes.

However, it would not do justice to the router, nor to cutter technology, to merely talk about 'a little going a long way' and mention only a few cutters. I have to remind myself that although I personally tend to design furniture in fairly 'straight lines' and happen to need only a few cutter profile shapes to achieve the visual simplicity I strive for, there are thousands of woodworkers who prefer decoration, ornament and the reproduction of period styles, to which the router equally lends itself, of course.

Fig. 3.3. Servicing cutters with the Trend Diamond Maintenance Kit.

It is possible to use the router to obtain virtually any desired profile shape in wood. Then you can compound different router cutter profiles to achieve more complex shapes, especially in architraves, etc, which are routed in more than one pass.

The technology is so complex and fascinating that it is not within the scope of this book to cover it all in depth, but here is a brief look at some of the main cutter types:

- straight flute cutters, single and twin (Fig. 3.6)
- ovolo and rounding over (Fig. 3.7)
- beads and reads (Fig. 3.8)
- chamfer 'V' groove (Fig. 3.9)
- radius and Cavetto (Fig. 3.10)
- dovetail (Fig. 3.11)
- slotting and grooving (Fig. 3.12)
- twist and dowel drills (Fig. 3.13)

Most cutters rely on the router and its fence

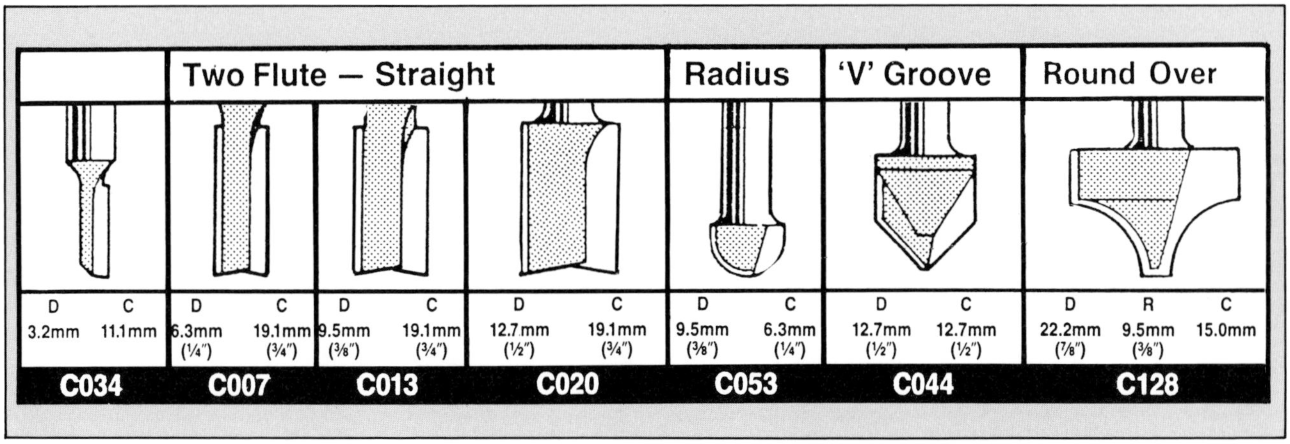
Two Flute — Straight
Radius
'V' Groove
Round Over
D C
3.2mm 11.1mm
D C
6.3mm 19.1mm
(¼") (¾")
D C
9.5mm 19.1mm
(⅜") (¾")
D C
12.7mm 19.1mm
(½") (¾")
D C
9.5mm 6.3mm
(⅜") (¼")
D C
12.7mm 12.7mm
(½") (½")
D R C
22.2mm 9.5mm 15.0mm
(⅞") (⅜")
C034
C007
C013
C020
C053
C044
C128

Fig 3.5. The Trend 'Craft Range' of 7 popular cutters.

or guide bush to guide the cutter, but there is a range of cutters in most profile shapes which are **self-guiding.** This is either achieved with a tiny **ball race** (and usually comes in a kit with two sizes of ball race), or as a **pin guide** integral to the cutter. In the case of the latter, care should be taken when operating to ensure the cutter is kept on the move, as any lingering in any one spot will cause a heat build-up and scorching of the wood.

Scorching of the wood is a common occurrence when routing. It is simply caused by lingering too long with the cutter, or by a combination of that and a dull cutter. The rate of feed or speed of 'pass' (speed at which you rout across the stock) is crucial and is also very difficult to be precise about in writing. It is rather like asking, 'What exact measurement are we talking about in order to achieve a tight wood-working joint?' – 1/1000th", 1/64th", or the thickness of a cigarette packet? You have to find out by yourself, through trial and error. (It is useful to remember that young children learn the most complex skills – tying up shoelaces, riding a bicycle, etc. – by trial and error. Most adults put a lot of emphasis on succeeding and cannot readily cope with failing, yet it *is* by failing that you build the necessary stepping stones for success!)

Cutters are very delicate and highly precise little objects. They are really quite

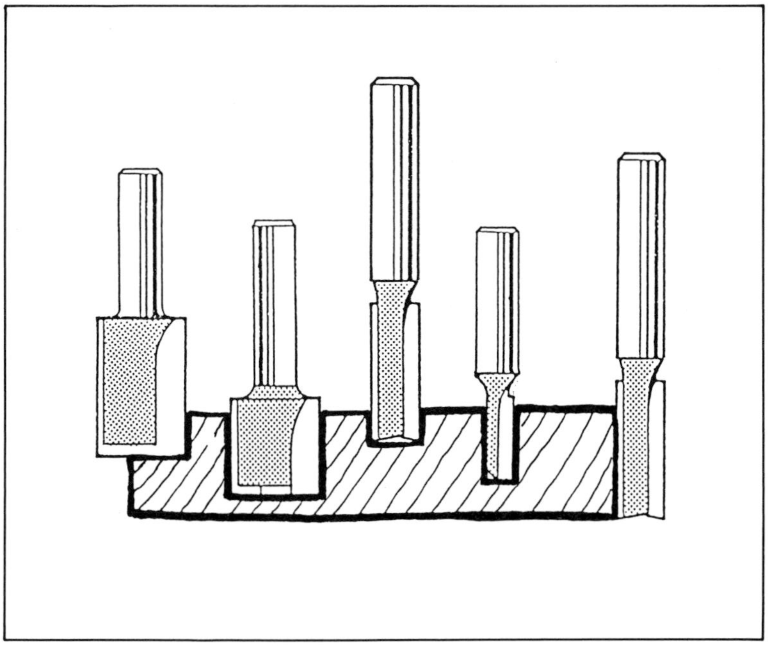

Fig. 3.6. Single and twin flute cutters for rebates, grooves and trimming (below, left).

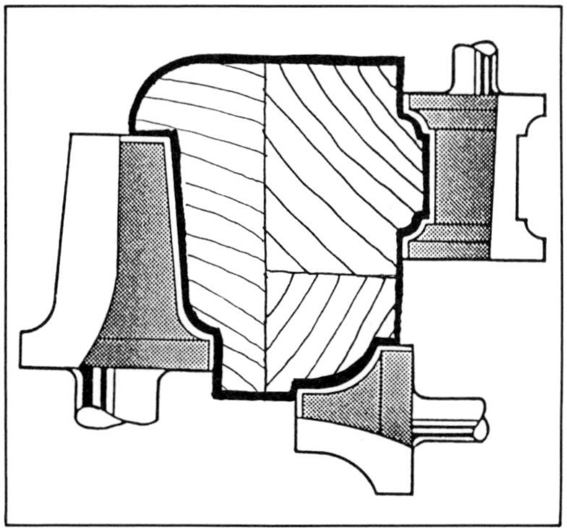

Fig 3.7. Ovolo and rounding over (below right).

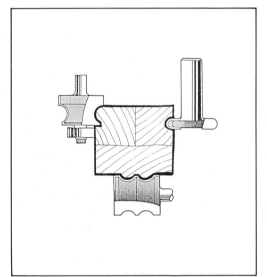

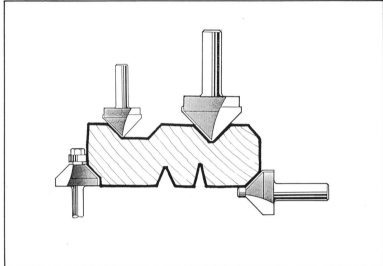

Fig. 3.8. Beads and reads.

Fig. 3.9. Chamfer/V-groove (above, right).

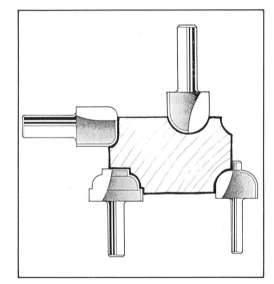

Fig. 3.10. Radius and cavetto.

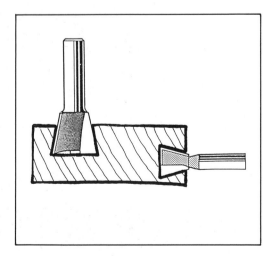

Fig. 3.11. Dovetail.

remarkable because of their relative small-ness and the incredible speed at which they fly round. Imagine that in the time it takes you to blink, that little cutter has rota-ted about 350 times – in other words, you just don't notice the speed it is going at. It not only does a lot of work extremely quickly, but it can also do a lot of damage equally quickly.

The **balance** of the cutter is of crucial importance, which is why any re-sharpening or servicing has to be done with great care. When honing a cutter you always work on the inside edge and never touch the outer profile. Like machine planer blades, both cutting edges should 'kiss' the wood simul-taneously. The very smallest cutters (under 3.2mm diameter) are single flute and there-fore balanced in terms of weight rather than weight and cutting stroke. The more efficient twin-flute cutters give a cleaner cut, and are highly precise with TCT edges carefully welded on. There are various grades of tungsten carbide and it is advisable to keep to the best for economy and safety reasons.

Cutters are extremely fragile and usually supplied in an oiled plastic coating for pro-tection. This can be easily removed with a Stanley knife.

It is always advisable to hold a cutter by

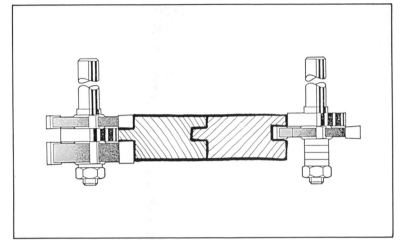

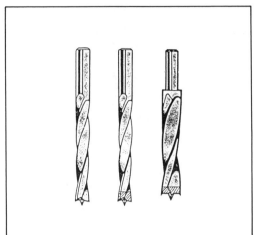

the shank, or if that is not possible, e.g. when removing it from the router, by the sides of the cutting edges.

It is easy to make a drilled storage rack to hold the shanks of your range of cutters. Each time I make a rack I try to anticipate the expansion of my collection by drilling extra holes, but they soon get filled up. As Andrew Varah says in the foreword, the cutters are soon worth more than the router! (It would make a nice router project to design and build a router box – see Little Boxes page 73.)

Care and maintenance of cutters is vitally important. The first lesson in any craft is maintaining the proper working order of tools. The thing about routing is that if the cutter is only slightly dull its performance deteriorates rapidly, causing the cutter to overheat, which in turn changes its molecular structure. Cutters are not cheap, and that alone should encourage the user to look after them. The only cutters I regard as 'throwaway' are the tiny 1.6mm straight cutters I use for making a 'Danish shoulder' (see page 135 of Circular Glass-topped Coffee Table, and page 184 of Roll-top Desk) on a piece of furniture. It is very difficult to avoid either breaking or burning them, but that may be because I have never enjoyed the luxury of an electronic router, where the revs can be dropped substantially to prolong the cutter's life.

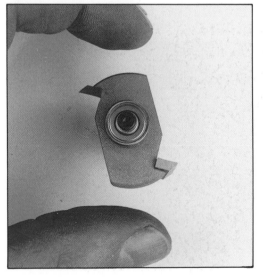

Fig. 3.12. Slotting and grooving (above, left).

Fig. 3.13. Twist and dowel drills (above, right).

Fig. 3.14. Cutters are usually supplied in an oiled plastic coating for protection.

Fig. 3.15. It is always advisable to hold a cutter by the shank.

Fig. 3.16. If the cutter cannot be held by the shank, hold the sides of the cutting edges.

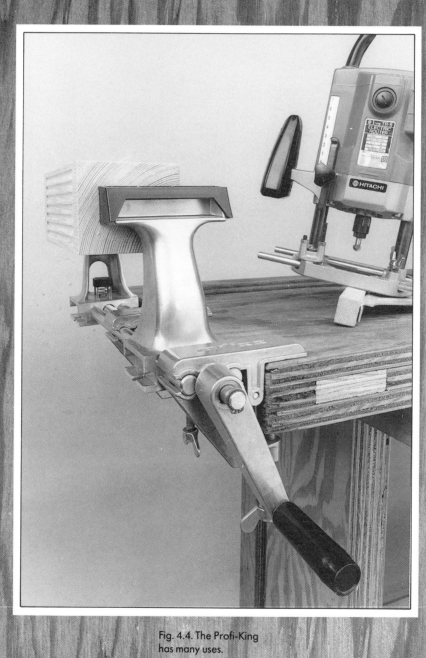

Fig. 4.4. The Profi-King
has many uses.

4 HOLDING DEVICES

The greatest holding device ever discovered is a **pair of hands!**

Throughout history the culture of the world has been 'handed down' – great architecture, engineering, literature, craftsmanship – all the product of hands.

The hands are probably still the ultimate holding device. (You only have to own a car like a Mini to realise how versatile the hands need to be when fumbling under the bonnet in such a cramped space trying to fix a bottom radiator hose!)

In routing operations, the hands are generally needed to hold the router when passing it over the wood, or vice versa. At this point I might add that my personal preference for the vast majority of routing operations is indeed to hand-hold the router.

This is mainly for two reasons. Firstly, through the machine I can feel the behaviour of the router, the cutter and the wood, hence giving me a greater control over the end result. Secondly, the stock is firmly held against the solidness of the bench rather than vice versa when the

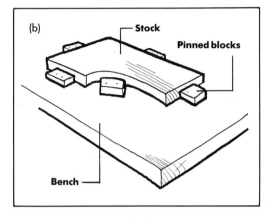

Fig. 4.1 (b). Pinned blocks as holding devices.

wood is held in the hands. This, of course, is a generalisation, and there are some operations which are best done on a router table where the wood is fed into the machine if a large surface area is required for support.

Because the router usually functions in connection with a jig such as a fence, guide bush, batten etc., there is often a problem as to how best to hold the work without the holding device fouling the router attachment. For example, the vice can interrupt the ride of the fence.

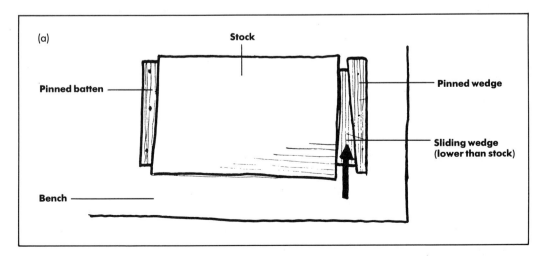

Fig. 4.1 (a). Wedges and battens as holding devices (plan view).

Fig. 4.2. The versatile G-clamp.

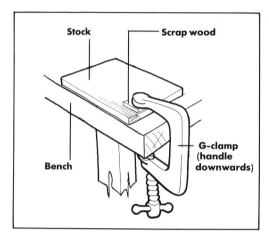

A little divergent thinking helps when considering how to hold the stock, rather than recourse to merely relying on clamps or vices. Here are details of some useful holding devices, involving both conventional and unconventional methods:

■ **Woodworker's Bench Vice.** Useful for short, narrow and thick stock. It is quick, but often limited in routing because the gripping action tends to get in the way of router fences etc.

Fig. 4.3. Sash clamps for holding long work.

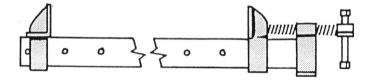

■ **Wedges, Cams and Pinned Blocks.** Simple improvised methods using scrapwood and panel pins, custom-made holding devices can be quickly built. Make sure the stock surface protrudes above the clamping system. (Figs. 4.1 (a) and 4.1 (b).)

■ **G-Clamps.** Used with scrapwood blocks (to prevent marking stock). This a versatile method of clamping and useful sizes are 100 and 150mm. Always position handles under the bench and out of the way and check router clearance. Stock is normally clamped to the bench (Fig. 4.2).

■ **Sash Clamps.** In various lengths and for holding long work end on. Can be supported in the vice (Fig. 4.3).

■ **Zyliss 'Profi-King' Clamp.** An ingenious and versatile bench-clamping system made of aircraft Duralumin with potential clamping configurations too numerous to show here. It is quick and strong and has the advantage of turning any reasonably solid table into a workbench. An ideal woodworker's 'mate' generally. (Figs. 4.4, 4.5, 4.6, 4.7.)

■ **Bench Holdfast.** Simple clamp which jams into a hole in a solid bench-top, gripping the stock on to the bench surface (Fig. 4.8).

■ **Dogs.** Used on continental style benches, fitting into positioned slots and operated by an end vice. This method is ideal as the gripping action is shallow and usually on the ends of the stock, and does not foul the ride of the router and its fence. Dogs are also a vital gripping method on the Black & Decker Workmate (Fig. 4.9).

■ **Black & Decker Workmate.** Hardly worth mentioning, because it appears on just about every other page of this book in conjunction with the projects! I consider it to be the ideal router's 'mate' because of its ingenious versatility. The wide opening table vice with varying angle positioning, together with four plastic 'dogs' over an array of holes, allows virtually any shaped stock to be held.

■ **Hot Melt Glue Gun** (by various manufacturers). If you are self-employed, this vastly underrated gadget serves as an extra pair of hands. I would not dream of using it to make permanent bonds in wood, but it is unbeatable for temporary fixing lugs in routing especially. The secret is to glue a small blob on the bench first, let it cool for a few seconds and then attach the stock. This way the stock is removed more easily afterwards without the grain being torn. Final cleaning up is done with a chisel. The 'hot-melt' action can therefore give a controlled bond by slight cooling. It is also useful for

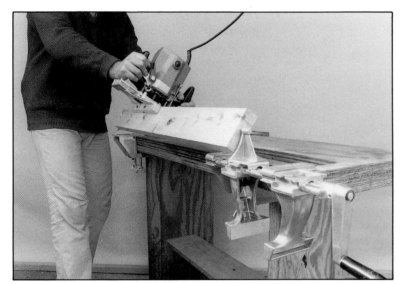

temporarily attaching MDF and similar templates on to the stock (Fig. 4.10).

Fig. 4.5. The Profi-King in another position.

■ **Doubled-Sided Tape.** Surprisingly effective; similar to carpet tape. If you apply enough of it the bond is sufficiently strong for joining templates to stock or stock to the bench-top.

■ **Specialist Clamps.** Trend Machinery & Cutting Tools supply a range of versatile clamps for specific routing operations, including toggle clamps, extended clamps, deep throat clamps, end socket clamps etc.

Fig. 4.6. The Profi-King yet again.

Fig. 4.7. The Zyliss Profi-King Clamp, an ingenious bench-clamping system.

Fig. 4.8. The bench holdfast, simple and effective.

■ **Dunlop Powerbase.** A system concept designed for general tools and materials handling, with some specific routing functions. It is described as a multiple guidance system for use with DIY portable power tools, drills, drillstands, saws, planers and routers etc. Its uses and versatility are too numerous to detail here, but its relevance to routing is a must. The comprehensive handbook is almost as thick as its table-top!

■ **Vacuum Holding Devices.** A simple and

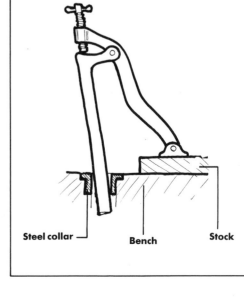

Steel collar   Bench   Stock

Fig. 4.10. Hot-melt glue gun – an extra pair of hands.

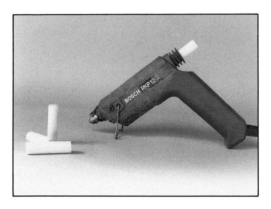

Fig. 4.11 (a). Specialist clamps from Trend (far right).

Fig. 4.11 (b). The Trend toggle clamp (far right).

Fig. 4.9. Dogs give ideal gripping action.

tant to use the 'air bypass' type (usually wet and dry vacuum cleaners) which avoids a build-up of pressure which would otherwise burn out the motor windings.

Simple vacuum clamps and chucks can be easily made from MDF or any manufactured board, some rubber or neoprene tube and plumbing connections and a closed cellular foam strip or roll (Fig. 4.12).

much underrated method of holding work. In most routing operations the holding device fouls the path of the router (e.g. a G-clamp can get in the way of the router fence), but in vacuum clamping the stock can be held down to the router table, for instance when overhead routing – either fixed head or by hand. Alternatively a vacuum chuck can be used, whereby both stock and template are simultaneously clamped under vacuum displacement to enable pin routing etc.

The method can be achieved either by using a purpose-built vacuum pump which displaces about 17psi, or by using a domestic vacuum cleaner for short periods; but in the latter case it is impor-

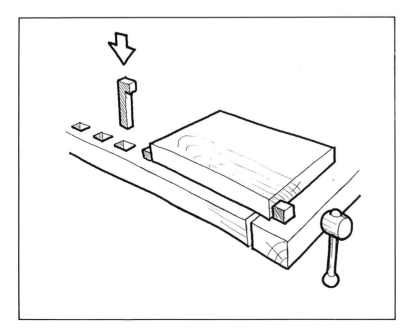

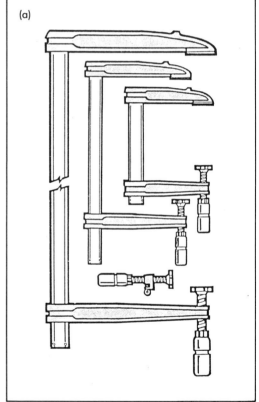

(a)

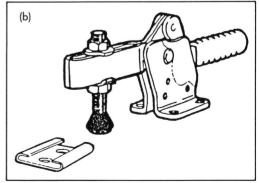

(b)

Fig. 4.11 (c). Trend's hold-down clamps with screw feed.

Fig. 4.12. A simple vacuum chuck.

Fig. 4.13. Section through a vacuum chuck used in inverted pin routing. (The router is overhead.)

There are one or two points to observe when vacuum clamping, and these are best illustrated by a diagram (Fig. 4.13).

These are just a few of the methods of holding down work. Because the potential of routing is so enormous, and the technology opens up countless new possibilities for the ways in which furniture and woodwork can be made, there are also numerous ways of holding the work. Everything depends on the particular situation, but for instance custom-made jigs can be of enormous assistance. This topic is dealt with in Chapter 6, and obviously there is an overlap of information.

By thinking out each holding problem in terms of its special requirements, and with the resources now available, there is no reason why the imaginative woodworker cannot find some effective way of holding down securely even the most awkward job. During my training days back in the early sixties double-sided tape, as far as I know, had not been invented – if it had, they never told me about it! This one simple method can solve numerous holding problems, so we are very lucky to have the benefits of the diverse technology described above today.

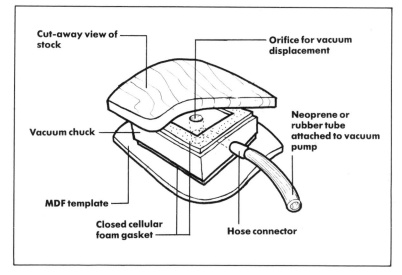

Cut-away view of stock

Orifice for vacuum displacement

Neoprene or rubber tube attached to vacuum pump

Vacuum chuck

MDF template

Closed cellular foam gasket

Hose connector

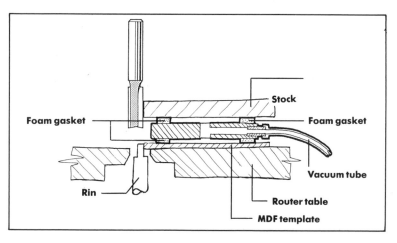

Foam gasket

Stock

Foam gasket

Vacuum tube

Rin

Router table

MDF template

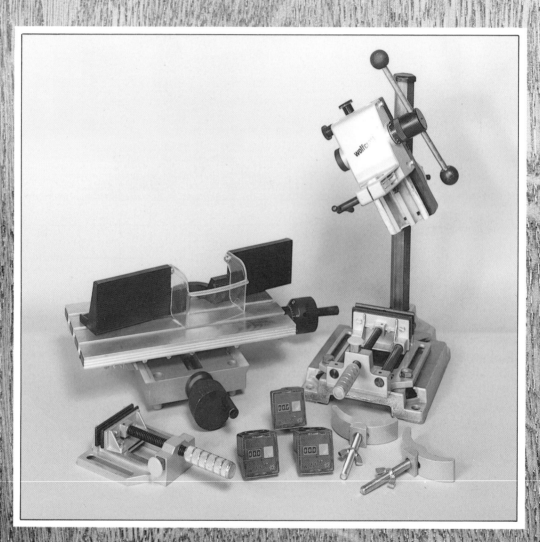

Fig. 5.10 Wolfcraft
Compass Drilling Stand
and Milling Table.

5 ACCESSORIES

Routing technology has given birth to an expanding industry in gadgets and attachments for the basic power tool. It is not my intention to cover in depth the whole spectrum (including the latest and greatest) in these pages, because this is essentially a creative projects book and such detailed information is excellently covered in several other router publications.

I have already mentioned a few important router accessories in Chapter 4 on Holding Devices, so there is no point in doing anything more here than mention them briefly by name: B & D Workmate, Zyliss Clamp, Dunlop Powerbase, various clamping devices by Trend Ltd.

Here are some brief details of a few relevant accessories which will help you to improve your creative routing:

■ **Elu Accessory Kit (E40900).** A wonderfully basic yet versatile kit of bits and pieces

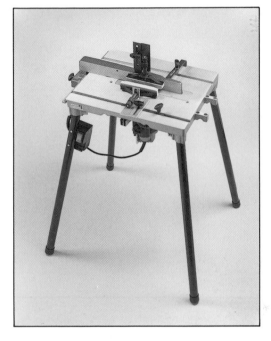

Fig. 5.1. Elu Combination Bench (551).

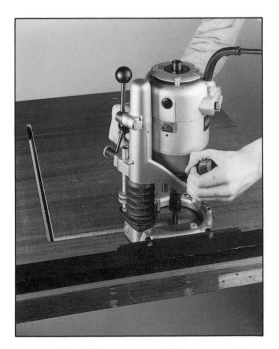

(about 20 separate components) which bolt together to make an inverted routing table or mini-spindle moulder. Its partner is the Elu MOF96 (750-watt) router, but any small router will fit by means of two rods passing through the router baseplate fence holes and into the table. The table can be mounted with quick release clamps (supplied) on to a plywood base board for mounting in the vice or workcentre. Pressure clamps help prevent the stock from wandering and the table can be turned on its side for joint cutting etc., with the wide fence acting as a base plate.

■ **Elu Combination Bench (551).** Also converts the router into a spindle moulder. It has optional fences, fine adjusters and pressure clamps (Fig. 5.1).

■ **Elu MOF112 Motor.** Extra heavy duty 2000-watt router motor for mounting on

Fig. 5.2. Elu MOF 112 Motor.

a three-column base (Fig. 5.2) or inverted or overhead table (T2). Such a motor would be ideal for use in a strengthened JKB copy carving jig (ideally made of metal, not wood).

- **Elu Dovetail Kit (E40001).** A fairly basic kit operated by the smallest routers to produce common and lap dovetails (Fig. 5.3).
- **Elu Minor Accessories.** Numerous small accessories ranging from extension base plates, ski sets, sub-bases, fences, fine height adjusters, trammel bars etc. too numerous to mention.
- **Elu Overhead Routing Machines (11/30, 11/32).** For machining wood, plastics, manufactured boards, pattern-making, milling and surfacing etc. Hand-lever and foot-pedal operated respectively.
- **Trend Routergraph Signwriter (12/30).** Pantograph style light carving and routing system. It will copy letters, signs, discs and other wood shapes on a 1:1 ratio (Fig. 5.4).

Fig. 5.3. Elu Dovetail Kit.

Fig. 5.4. Trend Routergraph Signwriter.

- **Trend Variable Frame Jig Set (Varijig).** Simple bar mechanism which has numerous possibilities for guiding a router and featuring parallel grooves quickly and accurately (Fig. 5.5).
- **Trend Ellipse Jig.** Enables virtually any router or jigsaw to cut ellipses. It can also cut circles.
- **Trend Guide Bush Sets.** Complete sets of 12 guide bushes in increments of 2mm from 10 to 32mm outside diameters (Fig. 5.6).
- **Portable Dust and Chippings Extractors (Trend, DeWalt, Kity).** A high priority for health and workshop cleanliness – but watch out your cutters do not disappear!
- **Trend Dust Extraction Fitments.** Central dust hoods, vented baseplate sets, hose and fittings etc.
- **Trend Lubricants and Materials (Diamond Maintenance Kit).** A diamond slurry solution which is applied on to a special tile from an aerosol can. Regular use will extend cutter life considerably (Fig. 3.3).
- **Manufacturers' Accessories.** All the router manufacturers (Black & Decker, Bosch, Hitachi, Kress, Elu, Makita, Ryobi etc.)

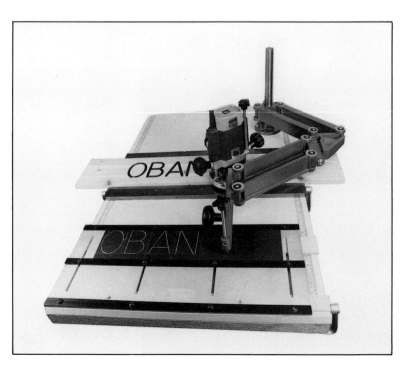

Fig. 5.5. Trend Variable Frame Jig Set.

supply specific router attachments for their particular routers, such as extra guide bushes, dovetailing kits, cutters etc. These are illustrated in their various product catalogues.

■ **Leigh Dovetail Jig.** A recent arrival on the UK market with great promise; probably the ultimate dovetailing jig, it is simple and quick to use once it has been set up and tested. It achieves the best-looking joints, with plenty of scope for individual tailoring and fancy dovetails. (See Chair project for its application.) Available

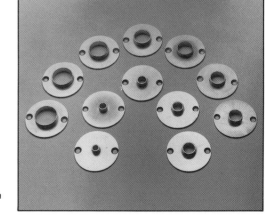

Fig. 5.6. Trend Guide Bush Set.

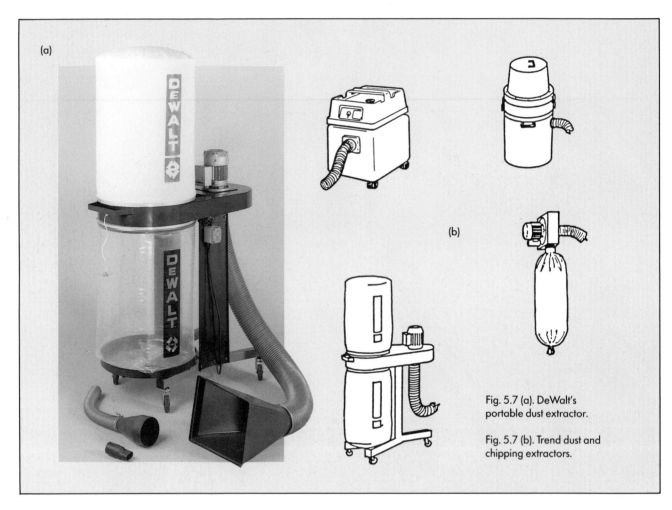

(a)

(b)

Fig. 5.7 (a). DeWalt's portable dust extractor.

Fig. 5.7 (b). Trend dust and chipping extractors.

from Sales & Marketing Services, of Silchester.

■ **Eumenia Radial Arm Saw/Router Attachment.** A lightweight precision system which allows radial arm routing. The basic saw frame can be used just with a router bracket attachment on to which most routers will secure. This offers an overhead router with vertical and horizontal adjustments, and the router bracket can be fixed or free riding to allow quick grooving.

■ **Vacuum Pumps.** For connecting up to a vacuum chuck or vacuum clamp system to hold work for routing.

■ **Wolfcraft Master Router and Drill Guide.** A very useful device for mounting the router drive motor in an angled jig.

■ **Wolfcraft Electronic Drillstand.** This versatile acessory has three LCD counters

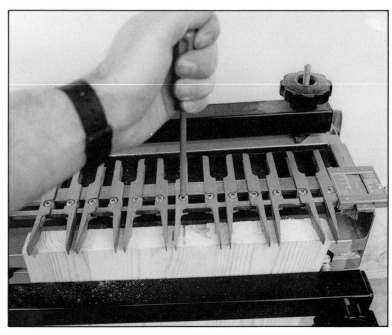

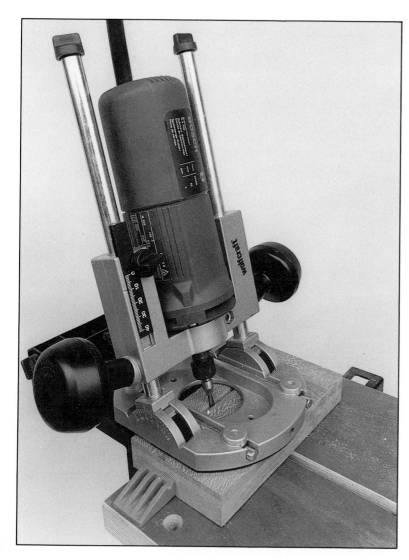

Fig. 5.9. Wolfcraft Master
Router and Drill Guide.

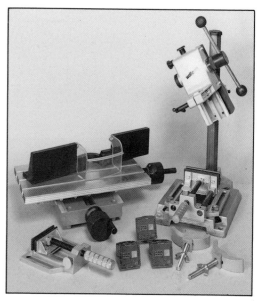

Fig. 5.10. Wolfcraft
Compass Drilling Stand
and Milling Table.

Fig. 5.11. Wolfcraft
Dovetailing Jig.

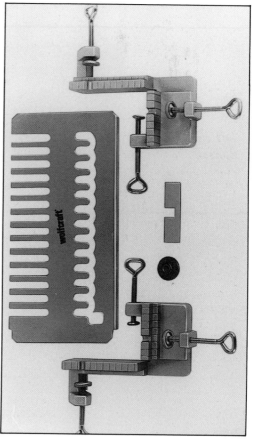

calibrating the movement of the column and milling table for real precision work. It also achieves angled cuts.

- **Wolfcraft Compass Drilling Stand and Milling Table.** Versatile drill and router stand with sliding table.
- **Wolfcraft Dovetailing Jig.** Simple and effective concept.
- **DeWalt (B & D) Router Attachment for Radial Arm Saw.** Provides the advantage of sliding the router head across the stock, in the same way as the radial arm saw blade behaves. This is a bracket attaching to the yoke.
- **Beall Power Screw Threading System.** See page 67.

Fig. 5.8. Leigh Dovetail
Jig (opposite).

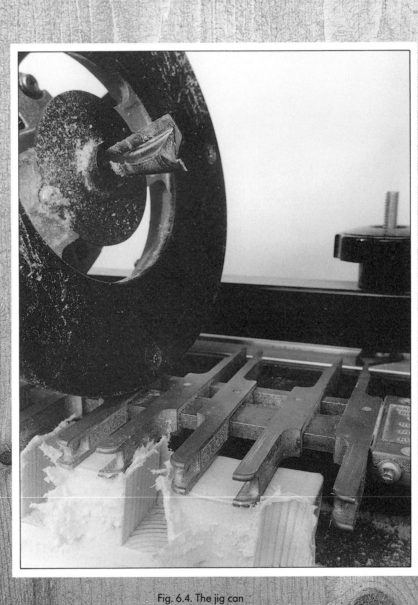

Fig. 6.4. The jig can function with a guide bush fitted to the router.

6 JIGMAKING AND MATERIALS

If cutter technology is at the heart of routing, then surely jigmaking is its very essence! This is probably the most creative aspect of routing. As already mentioned, you can clock up a lot of 'creative mileage' by using just a few cutters, but once you start making jigs the possibilities are never ending.

It is here that router technology really takes off, and the fascinating thing about it is that you can improvise with the most basic

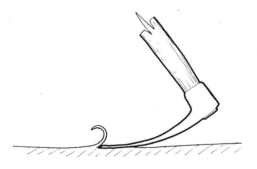

kit of materials and yet achieve the most complex routed operations.

In the history of furniture making the jigs which produce the objects are as important as the objects themselves. One is a means to the other. In these pages I can only hope to whet your appetite for this vast subject and offer you a basic survival guide. But if you really want to put your router into the fast lane, then start making jigs!

First of all, what is a jig? Apart from being a lively dance it is: the handle which holds a fretsaw blade; all the parts of a smoothing plane which enable the cutter to produce a fine shaving; one of the oldest woodworking tools – the adze, which by its very shape determines the cut it makes (Fig 6.1). These are examples of jigs; what is interesting about the adze, in particular, is that it is a good example of a self-guiding jig.

In routing terms **a jig is simply a guiding system to determine the path of the cutter**, and in some cases to hold the work as well. As I said previously, the router itself is a jig in so far as it controls the path of the cutter both vertically and horizontally (a straight fence is a jig, so too is a guide bush), and jigmaking generally just extends this notion. A routing jig can be a flat sheet template or a more complex device comprising several components.

The most basic jigmaking 'survival kit' is as follows:

■ MDF and plywood sheet material
■ a glue gun (hot-melt glue)
■ an attitude of mind!

This last ingredient is perhaps the most important and the most difficult to describe, as it involves the ability to design, invent and improvise. It is the way in which you **approach** the solution of technical/creative problems which is important, and this can only come about by first identifying the problem, then considering all the possibilities as to how it might be solved. You need an open mind rather than relying on traditional solutions.

Observation is a useful key, because many solutions are not 'original' but are applied elsewhere, and it's just a question of opening up our minds.

Jigmaking for the router should be considered as integral to routing techniques (which are covered in Chapter 7). Broadly speaking, the jig is a holding, steadying or guiding device which directly attaches to or feeds against:

■ the stock
■ the router base (or head) – see JKB Copy Carving Jig project and Fig. 6.2.

Fig. 6.1. The adze is a self-guiding jig.

47

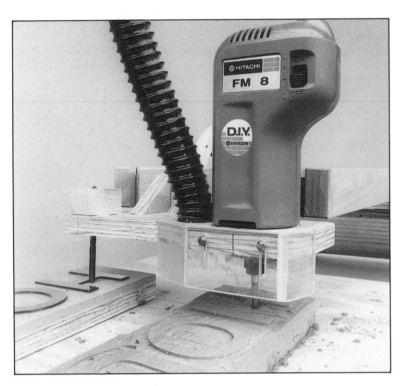

Fig. 6.2. The JKB Copy Carving Jig in action.

During the time when various router accessories were loaned to me, I had the embarrassing experience of ploughing a razor-sharp router cutter into the aluminium 'finger' of a costly dovetail jig. As I explained to the supplier, the collar depth of one particular manufacturer's guide bushes is not consistent, and in changing the cutter and subsequent guide bush the latter did not make contact with the aluminium jig (which in any case was lower than the base of the router), thus resulting in a wandering cutter. (Fortunately the 'fingers' were detachable and therefore replaceable at no great cost.)

When making jigs and templates, it is safer to ensure the jig makes contact with the base of the router; normally when using

■ the edge of the router base (Fig. 6.3), or
■ a guide bush fitted to the router (Fig. 6.4).

When considering specific jig constructions, it is worth looking at the requirements of each guiding method. For instance, the use of jigs and templates which rely on a fitted guide bush for their operation should take into account the outer diameter of the guide bush and the height of the collar (Fig. 6.5).

Fig. 6.3. The jig can attach to the edge of the router base.

guide bushes the thickness of the jig/template material should be about 6mm, which allows for the amount of recess the guide bush has when fitted to the router base (Fig. 6.5).

Another important dimension to note when guide bush routing – and one which is determined by the cutter diameter and the guide bush diameter – is the distance from cutter edge to guide bush collar outer edge. This is crucial (Fig. 6.6). The majority of manufacturers supply a standard 18mm guide bush which is an excellent size for most operations. There are optional sizes available (Trend supply a kit of bushes

ranging from 10 to 32mm in 2mm increments.) A typical router manufacturer's optional accessory set such as Hitachi (Fig. 6.7) consists of three different diameter guide bushes (20mm, 27mm and 30mm outside diameter), accommodating different-sized cutters. There are no strict rules about how snugly the cutter should fit inside the guide bush, but when using dovetail cutters be wary when you set the depth – if the plunging lock is suddenly released, the

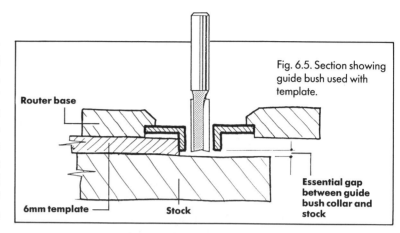

Fig. 6.5. Section showing guide bush used with template.

Router base

6mm template

Stock

Essential gap between guide bush collar and stock

Fig. 6.6. The distance from cutter edge to guide bush collar outer edge is crucial.

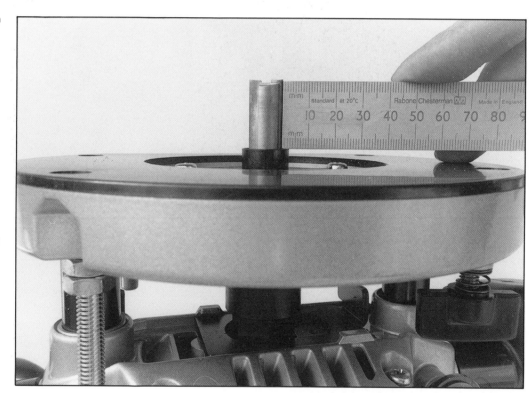

Fig. 6.4. The jig can function with a guide bush fitted to the router. (opposite).

Fig. 6.7. Hitachi's optional guide bush.

tapered cutter can foul the guide bush collar.

When making a guide bush template out of 6mm MDF or similar, the profile of the template must be smaller than the intended cut because of the above guide-bush-diameter/cutter-diameter relationship. It is easy to get confused, but I code each template with the appropriate cutter and guide bush diameters for safety.

The only remaining consideration is the method of fixing the template to the stock (also covered in Chapter 4, Holding

Fig. 6.8. The template fixed to the stock with double-sided tape.

Devices). Fig. 6.8 illustrates a 6mm MDF template attached to the stock with double-sided tape for edge trimming with a straight cutter and guide bush. The stock itself is mounted in the Workmate with a hot-melt mounting lug (easily removed afterwards). Notice how the shop-made dovetail jig uses the Workmate to grip both jig and stock in one operation (Fig. 6.9).

The advent of the **hot-melt glue gun** has revolutionised woodworking in so far as it 'takes the waiting out of wanting', and I suspect it is vastly undervalued as a workshop aid. I find it ideal for jigmaking and other temporary fixings. Personally I would not use it for cabinet work or for gluing together any of the projects in this book, as it lacks fibre penetration, but as a 'spare

pair of hands' and instant bonding agent for jigmaking it is unbeatable.

You may also wish to consider using PVA or other **wood glues** in conjunction with **screws** or **pins.** Panel pins (which have a 'lost head') are quite suitable and serve as a clamping device for the glue bond. One has to look at methods which work rather than relying strictly on tradition. I was taught never to screw into end grain, never to rely on an end-grain glue bond and always to line the screw heads up on a hinge! Of course these rules are well-founded, but there is a world of difference between making a tomato box and a jewellery casket.

Jigmaking has to be as accurate as that supreme craft – pattern making – but using the tricks of the carpentry trade. I am sure I have made my point.

The reader may be surprised to learn that the Universal Router Table and Copy Carving Jig were quickly built using a glue gun! It was my intention to use this method as a quick-build sequence for getting the jigs working, then to pull them apart and re-glue with PVA and screws, but it served perfectly well as a prototype for the projects in this book although I shall in due course improve the construction.

A range of **manufactured boards** (hardboard, chipboard, plywood and MDF) are suitable for jigmaking. My preference is MDF and plywood, taking both hot-melt glue and PVA and pins. I normally buy slightly damaged sheets in 8' × 4' sizes. Often it is a case of using whatever material is at hand, and utilising offcuts from larger projects.

The other tools of the trade I use for jigmaking are (for marking out):

> steel rule, tape measure
> try square, roofing square, set square
> ballpoint pen.

For making the jigs I tend to use:

> the bandsaw (or jigsaw if the wood is too large)
> machine planer and hand smoothing plane.
> finishing sander or table-mounted disc sander.

In the sense we are considering, the simplest jig is probably a **straight batten,** because it guides the path of the router in any desired straight line across the stock (and along its edge) and is particularly useful for end-grain trimming. Battens can be made of any straight-grained wood, preferably not plywood because it is difficult to get a perfectly smooth edge, and if the grain direction is 'short' the batten is inclined to bow. Ideal materials are beech or mahogany, but common pine will suffice.

A table I designed and made in 1976

(see page 1), from reclaimed pitch pine with a black acrylic inlay, used a batten exclusively for the routing of the 'cross-halving joints' in the top. You can't get a jig much simpler than that! Thin strips of wood were inlaid into one set of grooves, finished flush, then the adjacent set of grooves routed and more strips inserted. This produced the jointing effect, but it is a visual illusion. It was probably the making of this table (which years later was requested for a royal viewing at Kensington Palace amongst a small collection of selected British pieces!) which inspired me to think

Fig. 6.9. A shop-made dovetail jig uses the Workmate to grip both jig and stock.

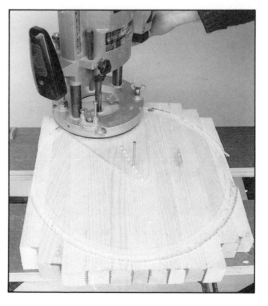

Fig. 6.10. It's easy to make your own circle-cutting jig.

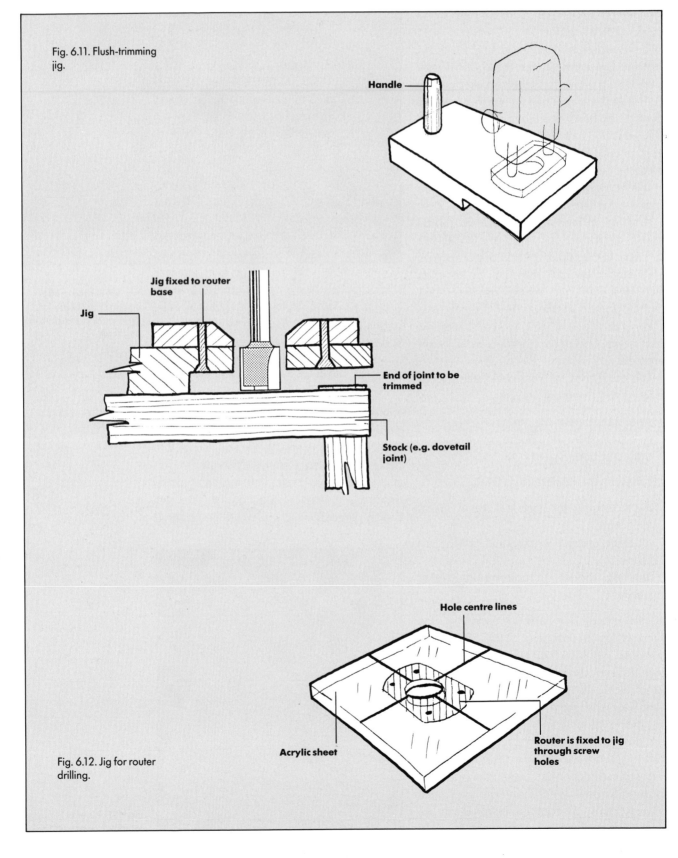

Fig. 6.11. Flush-trimming jig.

Handle

Jig fixed to router base

Jig

End of joint to be trimmed

Stock (e.g. dovetail joint)

Hole centre lines

Acrylic sheet

Router is fixed to jig through screw holes

Fig. 6.12. Jig for router drilling.

52

of the router as an immensely creative tool – yet a simple straight batten was used with my old Makita router.

From the simple batten we can proceed to consider jigs which attach to the base of the router, of which the straight fence and wheel guide are standard accessories. An example which springs to mind is the trammel for scribing circles. It is easy to make your own **trammel** or **circle-cutting jig** from MDF or clear acrylic (Fig. 6.10).

A useful jig for attaching to the router base is for **flush trimming** (Fig. 6.11), which is simply made from MDF or similar material.

I have mentioned elsewhere that the router can be used as a drill, but one problem is the router wandering slightly when operated and also in lining up the centre of the cutter. A simple **clear acrylic jig** with horizontal and vertical axes scribed on it can be attached to the router's base and lined up over a large marked cross representing the centre of the hole (Fig. 6.12). When using a router drill stand, the cutter can be lowered with its hand lever gently and accurately into the stock.

There are numerous extensions or jigs which can be attached to the base of the router for specific tasks, and secured by using the holes in the router sub base for threading through CSK bolts.

Jigmaking has figured largely in the design and making of the projects in this book, many of which rely on a specifically designed jig as the means of construction.

Let us consider one or two of these and how they came about. Pehaps the most challenging (or frustrating) was the 'end on end' dovetail template for the Coffee Table project (see Fig. 20.9). This jig is extremely simple but its accuracy is crucial. There was no other way than by trial and error to get the jig to cut tight joints, but the greatest cost was in time as the materials outlay was negligible.

Simplicity is usually the best solution, and it was possible to achieve two cutting operations using the same jig. The fixing lug holds the stock and in turn is held in the vice (Workmate). Ideally, for repeated use, the jig should be made out of a tougher material than MDF, say Tufnol sheet, which will wear much better, but for 'one-offs' and limited repeats MDF is quite suitable.

Another interesting jig used in this book is for cutting the 'fingers' for the 'rout-kerf joint'. This joint is quite tricky to make (there is a detailed account of the procedure in the Stool project) because the bend of the

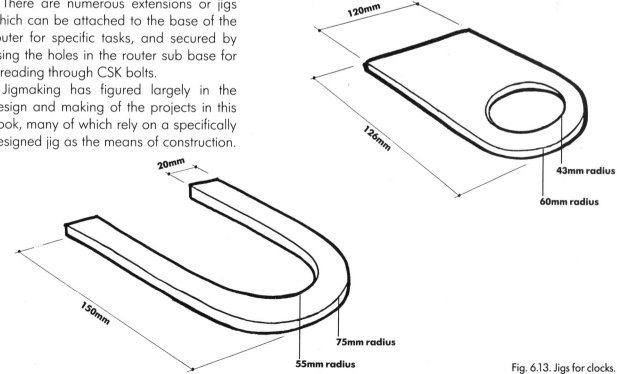

Fig. 6.13. Jigs for clocks.

wood relies on a very thin stock material which could easily break during handling. The right-angle jigs (Figs. 17.11 and 17.12) keep the stool firmly aligned until the finger-jointing jig replaces it, because it not only positions the router at 45 degrees to cut a long groove but also keeps the stool structure at a 90 degree angle at the same time, so it is of dual-purpose use. In designing it there were various problems to solve; as well as those just mentioned, a **guiding system** was needed for the router to track a straight grooved cut. I decided to build shallow walls at exactly the width of a chosen router (Hitachi TR12), which also acted as reinforcements to the sides of the jig. Therefore, once more several problems are resolved in one solution, keeping the jig as simple as possible.

One of the simplest jigs which offers a little creative potential is the one made for a clock (Fig. 6.13). This simple circle cut out of 6mm MDF allows a groove to be cut (using a guide bush with the router) or a shallow recess with straight or curved

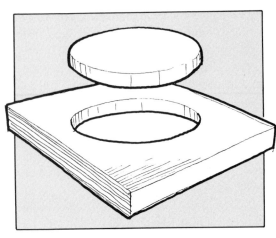

Fig. 6.15. Jig for rotating a dish on the pendulum jig.

Fig. 6.14. A simple circle guiding jig used in conjunction with the pendulum jig.

edges, depending on which cutter(s) you use. A similar but larger jig could be used for making dishes or plates.

Just as various complex cutter profiles can be achieved (composite shapes) by routing the different cutters in progressive passes, so too can complex routing operations be achieved by **composite jigging**. A good example of this is the jig for cutting the features of the chesspieces in the Chess Set project (Fig. 10.10). This jig is very

simple; it has a main body and two interchangeable parts – a straight template and an angled one. It successfully cuts the features of the five different chessmen, but although extremely simple it took some working out, I can tell you!

The problems were:

■ How to design symbols on the chess men which could be easily identified (the symbols graphically represent the moves of each piece, e.g. the knight which is symbolised by an 'L' can move three squares in and one to the right or left, or one square in and three to the right or left).

■ How to rout these symbols effectively with a standard cutter while maintaining material strength (fibre support) and visual clarity.

■ How to support the 30mm square pieces during routing, and hold them tight.

■ How to guide the router cutter accurately on such a small scale.

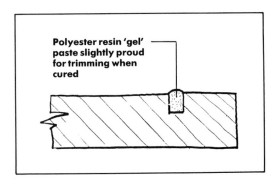

Polyester resin 'gel' paste slightly proud for trimming when cured

Fig. 6.16. Section showing resin inlay.

54

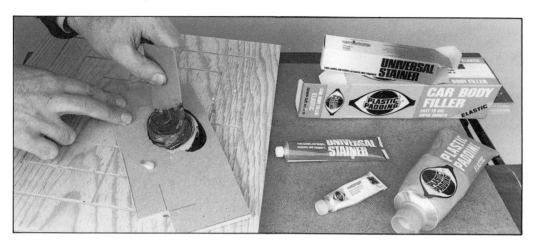

Fig. 6.17. Router inlaying with a pigmented paste based on GRP.

■ How to avoid grain tear at the end of the cut.

■ How to support the jig.

■ How to build the jig easily and operate it quickly.

This is the essence of jigmaking – identifying and understanding all the problems before you start (list them), and searching for the simplest solution (sketches). The design of the chess pieces and the jig for the chessmen took about a day to figure out.

I wonder how they originally got the adze to work? Was there a problem to be solved? Did it happen by accident? Or did it evolve slowly over a period of time and usage?

Another interesting jig used in this book is a simple **circle guiding jig** used with the **pendulum jig** (see Universal Routing Table project and Shallow Dish project, Fig. 6.14). Made of melamine-faced chipboard, it comprises a circular blank fitting exactly within an identical holed blank. Obviously it has to be made from two pieces to obtain the perfect fit, and the router can be used with a trammel guide to cut each circle accurately. This stock is mounted on the circle blank with a glue gun, and the hole blank is glue-gunned to the router table top exactly under the cutter of the pendulum router arm in its vertical position. The jig enables the stock to be rotated step by step in order to achieve the shallow concave dish (Fig. 6.15).

Now it was made of melamine-faced chipboard in preference to MDF for two reasons: the melamine offers an 'easy release' bond for the glue gun, and the chipboard rough edge is used to advantage – it acts as a friction surface for the routing operation as each rotation step has to be fixed for the router path. MDF would have been too smooth.

This reinforces the point about thinking out the specific problems of each jig, and in this case understanding the nature of the material (you never stop learning in this craft!). The jig is so simple, yet (with the equally simple action of the pendulum routing technique) it achieves some of the most fascinating router woodcraft.

A similar circle-guiding jig was used in the Breadboard project for guiding the cutter for inverted routing the edge and concave feature of the board (Fig. 15.10).

Moving on to other **materials** used in routing generally, we cannot totally divorce the craft of routing from the field of woodworking. Like any other tool (chisel, saw, etc.) the router relates to a vast technology which we piece together rather like a jigsaw puzzle – and still find we cannot complete the picture!

Understanding the nature of the material, its character and limitations, is essential for successful craftsmanship and design. When you consider that the term 'plastic' covers an infinite variety of materials with different properties and applications it is more aptly an adjective than a noun. Virtually the same applies with the term 'wood'.

Routing is peculiar to woodworking because it will do virtually anything in wood: it can *almost* bypass or ignore the character of the material. Many older craftsmen brought up on hand tools will understand what I mean. The carpenter's wheelbrace will slowly chew into the wood, giving the craftsman a direct experience of the nature of the material – as with a handsaw, spokeshave etc. – whereas the highspeed drill or circular saw will just 'do the job' in a flash.

At its crudest the only hint of the character of the material which routing gives is the smoke which pours out of the groove which has been 'attacked' with the router! Because it cuts wood like butter the router is an incredible tool which can be used on virtually any material – softwoods, hardwoods, manufactured boards, plastics, aluminium etc.

The main considerations are:
■ the resistance of the material to the cutter (density of material).
■ resin build-up (it sticks to and clogs the cutter, causing rapid wear).
■ the material fibre structure (close-grained or splintery).

When considering the density of solid woods, we tend to think of hardwoods and softwood. However this is only a loose classification, as some hardwoods are very soft (balsa wood) and some softwoods very hard (pitch pine)! The best guide is to dig your thumbnail into the surface. When using some of the harder woods, and in particular manufactured boards, it is wise to use TCT cutters for prolonged life. Routing non-ferrous metals and alloys like aluminium is best done with special cutters; acrylic in particular should be routed at a slow speed, otherwise it will melt!

While considering plastics, it is worth mentioning the use of **polyester resin** both as a waterproof high-build surface coating material (see the Drainer project) and as the main ingredient for resin inlaying (Fig. 6.16).

Polyester resin is the P in GRP which is popularly known as 'glassfibre' – glass reinforced polyester (not plastic). The resin with its chemical catalyst is the bonding agent and the glass strands give it the strength. It is used for boat hulls, car bodies etc. By using GRP with a **filler** (talc powder, calcite) you thicken the treacle-like liquid into a paste or gel; a readily available version of this is car-body filler (Plastic Padding, or David's Isopon; Plastic Padding also do a wood filler). By adding Universal Stainer to the mix, you can achieve a range of pigmented filler pastes ideal for router inlaying (Fig. 6.17).

Bear in mind that it shrinks and absorbs into the grain slightly and usually needs two applications. In three or four minutes it cures sufficiently for easy cleaning up with a plane or chisel (see Morris Nine Men Game project). The thickness of the paste is crucial to the degree it sinks into the grain. If it is too runny, it weeps into the grain and does not give a clean inlaid line.

MDF is an ideal material for jigmaking because of its consistent density on both surface and edge. Most manufactured boards (chipboard, plywood, hardboard) have a rough edge and particularly in the case of chipboard it needs further treatment (lipping) (Fig. 6.18).

It is claimed that when spray lacquering MDF it will take to the edge, which is quite remarkable for a fibre board which is of a compressed nature. However, the advantage in jigmaking is that MDF has an edge sufficiently stout and smooth to use 'undressed' as a template and jig material.

That is not to say that other manufactured boards cannot be used in jigmaking. I have numerous router jigs and templates made of ¼" **hardboard** which are still in service but were built before MDF was available.

Finally, a look at some other materials

used in routing and in the projects section of this book:

Abrasive Paper. I use this term broadly as it covers aluminium oxide paper, carborundum paper, garnet paper, glasspaper, flour paper, Wet & Dry paper, Lubrasil paper etc. (but definitely not 'sandpaper' – there is no such thing, it is not made from sand).

Abrasive papers are supplied in different 'grit' ratings. As a general guide, the medium-coarse to medium grades are sufficient for most work, with fine smoothing achieved with flour paper or Lubrasil paper. It can be purchased in sheets, or in rolls if you are using a large quantity. Though expensive, Wet & Dry paper is very effective for final finishing and of course is used 'dry'.

Glues. The hot-melt glue gun with glue sticks is ideal for jigmaking, but for more permanent bonds it is best to use PVA (poly vinyl acetate) glue, which is widely used in the woodworking industry. It should be bonded under pressure and normally cures in about two hours at room temperature, or overnight for curved laminated work. Cascamite is a good all-purpose glue, mixed four parts to one of water; it has a longer pot life than PVA, and takes about eight hours to cure in clamps.

Screws and Pins. Screws are of three basic types – countersunk (CSK), round head and raised head – and are supplied in mild steel, brass or black enamelled in the case of round heads. CSK screws are the most common, requiring a pilot and shank hole to be drilled. When using brass screws, always pilot first with a steel one as brass is brittle. Panel pins ranging from ½" to 1½" are useful for jigmaking in particular, as they have a lost head and cause minimal splitting in narrow-edged boards. They tend to bend if the material is dense.

Finishes. This is an entire subject on its own, but I shall deal with some basic finishes used

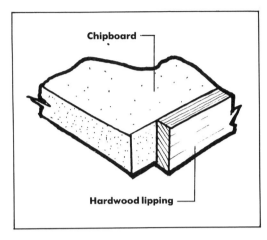

Fig. 6.18. A hardwood lipping protects the edge of the chipboard, allowing edge treatment and finishing.

in the projects section.

Linseed oil (neat or slightly diluted with turps) is a lovely finish for several timbers such as oak and elm, but not so effective for others such as ash.

Polyurethane varnish is much scorned by many 'experts' (I think it is the name rather than the job it does). By diluting the first coat slightly and applying perhaps two to three coats only (matt varnish) a serviceable, attractive and durable finish can be achieved. I have used polyurethane stained varnishes in the projects section (Chess Set project) with effect. One coat of clear is applied first, followed by one or two coloured coats; like clear polyurethane varnish, it takes about eight hours to fully cure. Brushes should be cleaned in turps.

Cellulose lacquer, thinned with acetate thinners, is usually sprayed on. It is very quick drying, and a perfect finish can be achieved by building up a number of sprayed coats. A sanding sealer should be applied first. You need good ventilation. It can be brush-lacquered, but you have to be quick as brush-marks show. Available in matt, satin and gloss.

Aerosol spray lacquers are particularly useful for small applications and are ideal for some of the projects in this book (see Clocks projects).

Many of these materials can be obtained from paint suppliers, DIY shops, car accessory shops and so on.

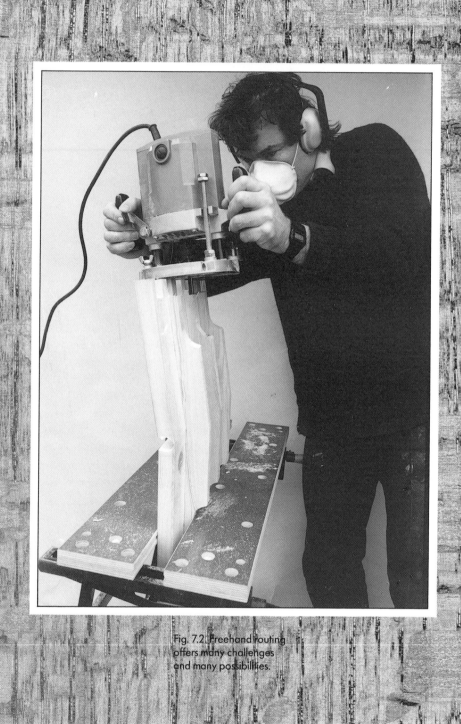

Fig. 7.2. Freehand routing
offers many challenges
and many possibilities.

7 ROUTER TECHNIQUES

Amongst my own collection of books are several which come under the general classification of 'reference' – books which I can quickly refer to in order to find out something I want to know, whether it's 'Improve your squash', 'Tuning Mini engines' or 'Dry fly fishing'.

To achieve a standard of excellence in any field demands a variety of skills, not least the mastery of that good old-fashioned term – **technique**. It crops up in every human endeavour, whether acting, playing golf or winning a law-suit.

Although I am a designer, I trained in cabinet-making techniques. Those techniques (learned largely at the bench) have provided me with the vital 'vocabulary' necessary to produce creative work, sometimes offering a springboard to explore new ways of fashioning the material. Perhaps the Stool project in this book (which utilises a new routing joint based on other woodworking traditions) is a good example (Fig. 7.1).

This book is about techniques which are delivered through a series of carefully structured creative projects; *this* chapter deals separately with those techniques, and also others not covered in the projects section, hence giving the reader a useful routing vocabulary.

Some of the techniques are dealt with in greater depth in the projects section in a 'hands on' way, so there is much cross-fertilisation throughout. It is not an A–Z, more a short ABC of routing techniques.

FREEHAND ROUTING

Perhaps the easiest and yet most difficult technique to master, since the user has to control the path of the router and its cutter as it journeys across the wood. There is less to think about, since there are no jigs or fences, but it demands a very steady hand and confident approach. I think this technique is the best way of gaining that confidence. The determining factors for successful freehand routing are a light- to medium-weight router, small-diameter cutter and shallow cuts (less resistance from the material). The method lends itself to carving, quick removal of stock and skilful trimming (Fig. 7.2). (See Table Mats and Little Boxes projects.)

FENCE ROUTING

Perhaps the most common technique. Achieved either with the standard accessory straight fence supplied with a portable router, or as a fixed fence on a router table. The principle is the same in each case. The fence is set at a fixed distance from the router cutter (either its edge or centre) and is guided against the edge of the stock in the same fashion as when using a marking gauge. The straight fence must be used against straight stock, ensuring the cutter

Fig. 7.1. The stool is an example of a new routing joint derived from other woodworking traditions.

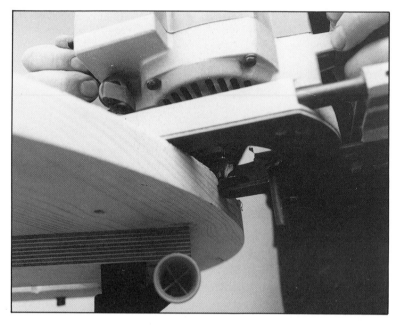

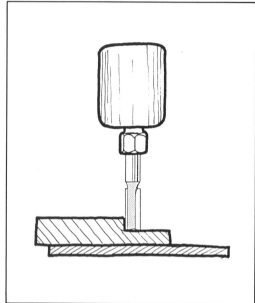

Fig. 7.3. Wheel guide routing enables curved-edge stock to be routed against.

Fig. 7.4. Table or fixed routing allows the wood to be supported throughout its entire journey.

Fig. 7.5. Overhead router, fixed head (above, right).

Fig. 7.6. Inverted router, fixed head.

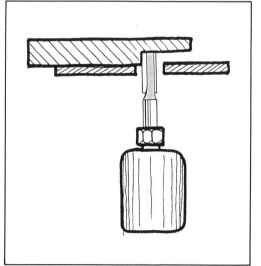

Fig. 7.7. Safe inverted routing.

follows a parallel path. The method is used for routing rebates and grooves. (See Mirror, Boxes, Chess Set, Morris Nine Men projects etc.)

WHEEL GUIDE ROUTING

Usually an attachment to the fence whereby a wheel or roller makes contact with the edge of the wood instead of the straight fence, enabling curved (concave and convex) edged stock to be routed against (Fig. 7.3). Care must be taken in setting the height of the wheel just below the cutter depth, but in good contact with the edge of the stock on narrow work. (See Coffee Table project and Fig. 2.6.)

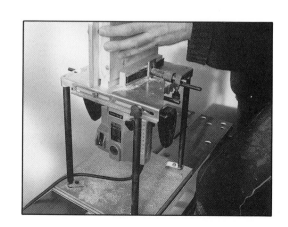

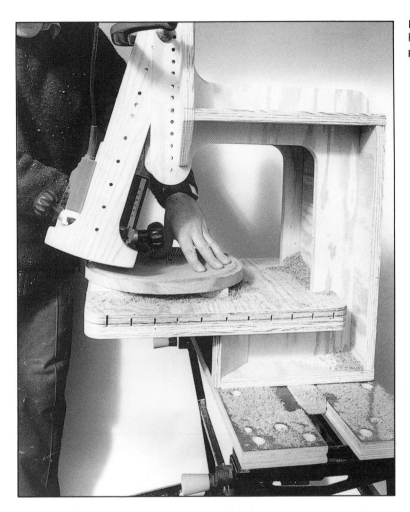

Fig. 7.8. Pendulum routing has numerous creative possibilities.

Fig. 7.9. Flush trimming. Set the depth of cut fractionally below the thickness of the template or jig.

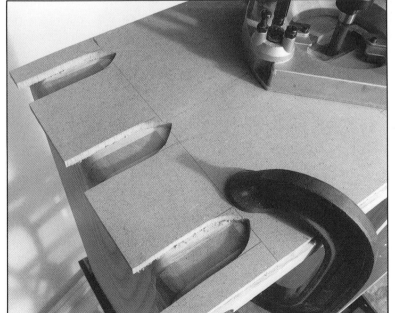

BATTEN ROUTING

A simple method with enormous creative potential. A straight-edged piece of wood is clamped on to the stock, with clamp handles downwards out of the way. The edge of the router base is run against the batten so that long cuts can be made, especially in the middle of large panels where the straight fence cannot reach. This method is used mainly for grooving. (See Morris Nine Men and Chair projects, etc.)

TEMPLATE ROUTING
(with guide bush)

This is probably the most creative and versatile method of routing. A range of small- to large-diameter guide bushes fit into the base underneath, usually by two screws,

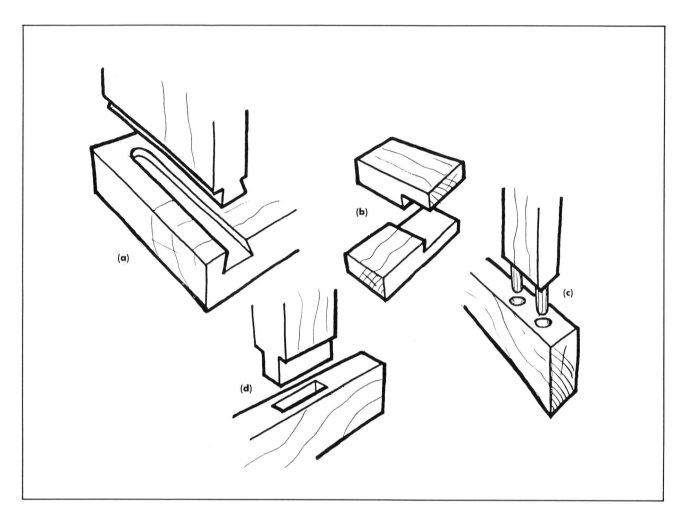

Fig. 7.10 (a) Dovetail housing joint. (b) Halving joint. (c) Dowel joint. (d) Mortise and tenon.

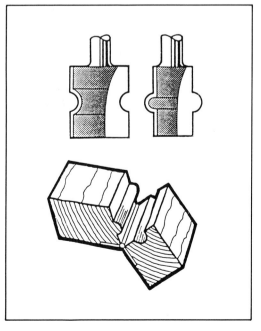

Fig. 7.11. Tongued/bead joint set and cutters.

and the cutter passes through the guide bush freely. A template of the desired edge profile is attached to the stock (usually 6mm MDF) and the lip of the guide bush follows its profile. This method is used for both groove and edge trimming operations and usually in conjunction with straight cutters (or dovetail cutters used with a variety of dovetailing jigs). Some older routers use a two-piece bush. The upper part screws into the actual threaded guide bush, thus overcoming the problem of holes in the router base. (See Clock, Chess Set and Chair projects and Fig. 6.4.)

FAST PLUNGE ROUTING

I mention this technique as although most routers plunge in their normal operation to achieve freehand, fence, batten routing etc., this is a very efficient method I use for quick removal of stock. Perhaps I should call it 'jump routing' as I have got it down to such a fine art that the router almost takes off! No sooner is it swiftly plunged than it is quickly spring released in a series of rhythmic overlapping cuts. I go into it in more detail on page 74 of the Box project, but this method removes the bulk of stock far more swiftly and efficiently than routing a series of shallow horizontal cuts in the conventional way. You probably won't find this method anywhere else. It is crucial to make crescent-shaped cuts (in section) hence minimising resistance from the material. This method allows fast chipping clearance on deep cuts. There is no other way! (See little Boxes project, Fig. 9.5.)

TABLE OR FIXED ROUTING

Where the router is mounted to a table in a fixed position and the stock passed over the table surface. The advantage of this method over hand-held routing is generally for straight-through cuts on small-sectioned timber where the wide table supports the wood in its entire journey (Fig. 7.4). There are two main types of table routing:

Fig. 7.13. The highly precise rule-joint cutters.

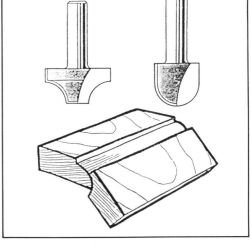

Fig. 7.12. Finger jointing can be put to decorative use.

Overhead Routing

Here the router is fixed in a rigid arm overhanging a table and is lowered on to the stock which passes across the table (Fig. 7.5). The stock is guided by any method such as fence, guide bush or a pin and template. More sophisticated tables have foot-controlled plunging mechanisms to allow the operator to use both hands to control the stock, otherwise a hand lever is used on the router head (Fig. 1.4). Notice the small pin on the router table; this is used as a guide against the template attached to the underneath of the stock. (See JKB Universal Router Table and Shallow Dish projects.)

Inverted Routing (Spindle moulding)

This is perhaps the most popular fixed routing method in the UK (Fig. 7.6). The router is mounted underneath the table, the cutter set to depth and the stock passes over the table against various guides, as mentioned above (including pinhead, with the pin fixed overhead). Inverted routing is commonly used in the woodworking industry on a larger machine and is called spindle moulding. It is used for edge profiling against a fence or template in straight and curved work. I would personally rate the spindle moulder as about the most dangerous woodworking machine, since its

Fig. 7.14. The biscuit jointer achieves a range of jointing configurations.

huge cutters are separately mounted into a cutter block and if not properly secured will fly out and cause havoc; although safety cutters are mostly used nowadays, its smaller routing companion is generally regarded as safer than the overhead router (Fig. 7.7).

With inverted routing the stock covers the cutter and in theory protects the user's hands – although you can't see what you are doing! With overhead routing you can see the cutter, but it is unprotected and dangerously near the user's hands. In my opinion *all* machines are potentially lethal. The main advantage of inverted routing is that if you are profiling and edging the table surface acts as a depth guide and the cut will be parallel. If you use an overhead router, the advantage is that you can see what's going on, but the accuracy of the depth of cut relies on the stock being parallel in thickness – which does not allow for a slightly bowed stock. (See JKB Universal Router Table, Coffee Table projects etc.)

PENDULUM ROUTING

An overhead method of routing whereby the router head is fixed in a cradle over the table, which swings on two pivot points. By lowering the cutter into the stock in shallow depth cuts, a concave cut is achieved. Or by rotating the stock in graduated steps, a circular cut can be made. This simple technique has numerous creative possibilities if other jigs are attached. The cutting arc can be varied and the swinging arm can

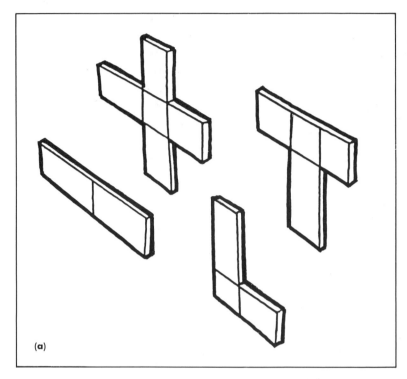

(a)

be fixed in an angled position and the stock rotated (Fig. 7.8). (See JKB Universal Router Table and Shallow Dish projects.)

TRAMMEL ROUTING

A simple technique for achieving circular cuts of any diameter for grooves, edge profiling and trimming. Either a commercial trammel or a shop-made one (Fig. 6.10) will suffice.

ROUTER DRILLING

The router is a drill, although normally used to translate circular holes into grooves or rebates. By keeping the router stationary it will plunge cleanly and accurately, making a cleaner hole than any drill, *provided* the router does not move. So either it has to be jigged up, or what I often do is attach masking tape to the underside of the router base to stop it slipping. A typical application of router drilling is to set the fence and drill a series of locating peg-holes for shelf adjusters on a bookcase, or for dowel jointing with a shop-made jig. (See Morris Nine Men project.)

Fig. 7.15. (a) The main joint configurations in woodworking: **X L T** and **I** connections. (b) **T X** and **L** joints in perspective.

FLUSH TRIMMING

A straight cutter with bottom cut is used (preferably 6mm diameter upwards) to trim edge joints etc. clean and flush by means of a very simple jig. This is so simple it can be just a piece of MDF with cut-outs for the joints and fixed to the stock (Fig. 7.9), or a similar jig fitted to the router base with clearance for the cutter. The crucial factor is to set the depth of cut *fractionally* below the thickness of the template or jig. (See Chapter 6, Jigmaking.)

JOINT CUTTING

This subject really warrants a chapter of its own. There is hardly a traditional wood-working joint that the router cannot achieve and furthermore it can create new joints (such as the JKB 'rout-kerf' described in the Stool project).

The most common joints — housings, half-laps, dowelled, and mortise and tenon (Figs. 7.10a–d) can be achieved by simple routing techniques and jigs/attachments (either standard accessory or shop-made), while the dovetail can be achieved with either shop-made or manufacturers' acces-

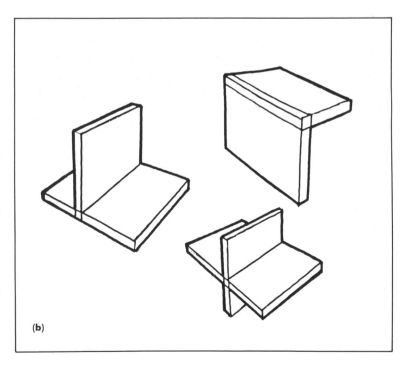

(b)

sories (Trend, Ryobi, Leigh etc., see Coffee Table project and Chapter 6 on Jigmaking).

Various cutters are specifically designed for jointing operations such as tongue and grooving sets (Fig. 7.11) (profile/scriber sets), finger jointers (Fig. 7.12) which I have put to decorative use in this book (see Bookends project) and cutters for the highly precise rule joint (Fig. 7.13) which only the most skilful craftsmen can make by hand.

BISCUIT JOINTING

This warrants special mention because it is almost a technology of its own. Any commercial woodworker who owns a biscuit jointer (Fig. 7.14) will wonder how they survived without it! It is really more a tiny circular saw than a router, but somehow comes under routing technology. The crescent-shaped woodfibre biscuits are set into matching cuts machined swiftly by the power tool against appropriate marks, hence achieving a range of jointing con-

Fig. 7.17. A router screw threading device.

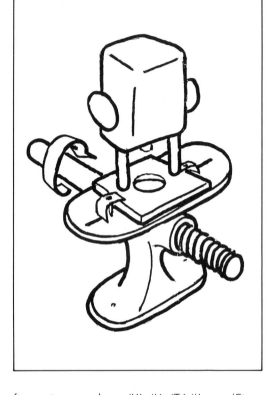

Fig 7.16. Dowel cutting jig.

figurations such as 'X', 'L', 'T,' 'I' etc. (Figs. 7.15(a) and (b).)

DOWEL CUTTING

The main trouble with manufactured dowel is that it is generally available in one timber only – ramin – other than the short manufactured dowel lengths with glue flutings which are made of ash. There are times when you need a non-standard dowel perhaps for decorative and structural use, and this is where the router comes in handy. A simple dowel cutting jig (Fig. 7.16) used in conjunction with a power hand drill can easily convert square or octagonal stock into dowel of any desired diameter and timber variety. The jig is ideally precision-made of steel.

ROUTER INLAYING

I mention this one because it features in the Projects section (see Morris Nine Men Game). It is also dealt with in Chapter 6 on Jigmaking and Materials. The technique

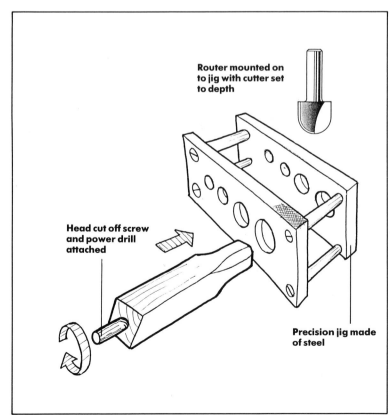

Router mounted on to jig with cutter set to depth

Head cut off screw and power drill attached

Precision jig made of steel

employs simple fence or batten routing to achieve the desired groove for an inlay. Instead of inlaying a contrasting timber, you use a thixotropic polyester resin pigmented with a colour. This simple and effective technique allows unusual inlay configurations together with the novel 'radiused corner' detail which expresses the router so clearly.

DANISH SHOULDER

This technique should not go unnoticed. It is the creation of a tiny gap (1.6mm) routed along the shoulder line of a joint which greatly clarifies and enhances it (see Rolltop Desk, Fig. 26.28). (This principle is not new. In Michelangelo's famous Renaissance painting of God creating Adam, the fingers of God and Adam all but touch, except for the most minute gap, creating enormous energy from the tension between the two figures.)

ROUTER SCREW THREADING

A technique with huge creative potential for cutting external and internal threads in wood of any diameter and any wood (preferably close-grained hardwoods). Some ingenious jigs have appeared in the American *Fine Woodworking* magazine.

The stock is usually rotated by hand and fed into the jig which has the router fixed to it (Fig. 7.17). Illustrated here is the Beall Power Screw Threading System (now available in the UK through Tillgear) which cuts external threads from 3/8" to 1" diameter (Fig. 7.18). (Some of the US jigs can cut much larger diameters and include internal threading, whereas this jig relies on an HSS tap for the internal thread.)

Fig. 7.18. The Beall Power Screw Threading System.

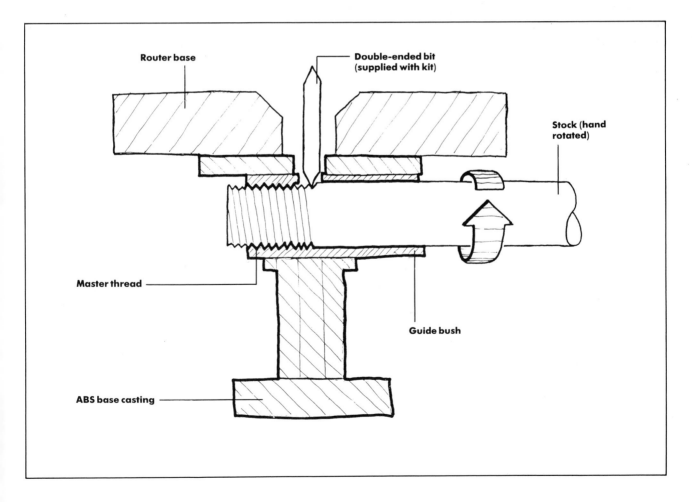

Router base

Double-ended bit (supplied with kit)

Stock (hand rotated)

Master thread

Guide bush

ABS base casting

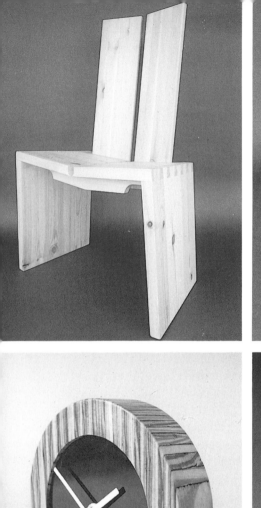

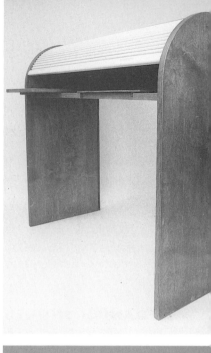
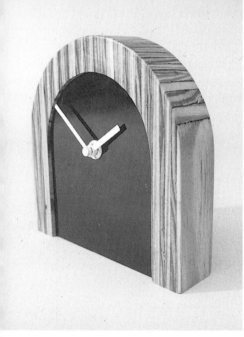

PROJECTS

When deliberating over what techniques I should deliver first through the range of projects in this book, a thought passed through my mind about the way I first learned to ski.

Several years ago a Canadian friend (a ski champion from Montreal) took me to Aviemore in Scotland – if you can ski there, you can ski anywhere! – and on the chairlift to the famous 'White Lady' run. I did not expect him to leave me stranded, but as he hurtled off down the slope ignoring my shouts he muttered something about keeping the toes pointed inwards and the knees together! Miraculously I got to the bottom of the mountain, with numerous falls and apologies to other skiers, but I had got a taste for the sport with little chance to let fear get the better of me, and I was immediately on the chairlift again.

Perhaps the best way to get a taste of this 'animal' is through freehand routing. You will quickly learn just how a router behaves, and therefore speedily establish the necessary confidence and control. The instant kick of the router starting up immediately tells you to take command, and indicates the firmness of grip required to cut a freehand pass when you plunge the cutter into the wood. You will feel exactly how the router tries to 'snatch' into the wood, and will soon learn to work at the rate of feed and depth of cut the tool requires.

TABLE MATS ★

Simplicity often wins the day and these table mats (Figs. 8.1 and 8.2) involve just one simple technique – **freehand routing.**

Made from solid teak or elm, approx. 150mm square × 25mm deep, the blanks are prepared to size, using hand tools or a planer–thicknesser if you have one. You can cut as many blanks as you require, and of course they need not strictly conform to this size.

The blank is held in the vice, or as I prefer, in the Black & Decker Workmate, using the dogs.

Any small- to-medium-sized router is ideal for this project, from 750 to 1300 Watts, although I used the Ryobi 2HP (R500) model.

A table mat is made as follows:

1 Secure the mat blank in the vice (I use a Black & Decker Workmate, with dogs).

2 Set up the router with a 12.7mm diameter two-flute cutter with bottom cut and set the depth stop to a fraction over half the thick-

Fig. 8.1. Table mats involving one simple technique: freehand routing.

Fig. 8.2. A graphic view of the table mats.

ness of the wood (13mm).

3 Set cutter to approx. 4mm depth and make a freehand pass straight across the centre of the wood blank. There is no need to mark it out with a pencil. Keeping a steady hand, slowly pull the router back towards you, allowing the line to be slightly wavy (this is the intention; if we wanted a dead straight line we would use the fence).

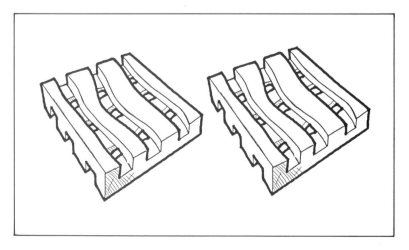

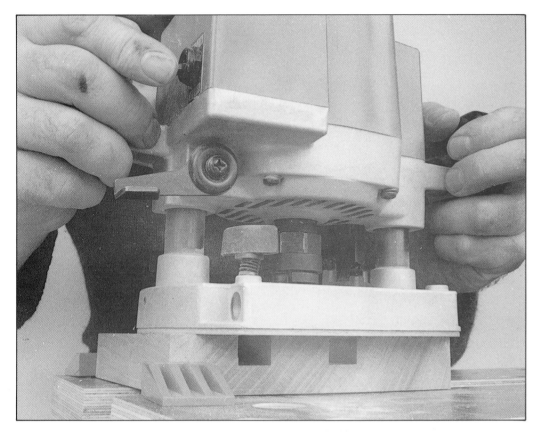

Fig. 8.3. Feel the cutter biting into the wood by keeping your hands firm on the router.

Fig. 8.4. Square holes appear as the first set of cuts is intersected.

4 Now lower the cutter by another 4mm and make another pass, trying to keep to the original line. It does not matter if you go off course slightly, but try to keep your hands firm on the router and *feel* the cutter biting into the wood (Fig. 8.3).

5 Make another pass, setting the cutter another 4mm or so, until it reaches maximum depth, and clean up the edges making sure there is a clean vertical edge on either side of the cut.

Now here is a test for you – the width of the cutter is 12.7mm and my cuts were kept to under 15mm; see if you can achieve that accuracy. It does not matter if they are wider, so long as they are clean, but it's

worth trying to get control of the tool right from the start.

6 Make similar cuts in between the central groove and each edge of the mat. This entire operation only takes a few minutes.

7 Reverse the mat and do likewise on the other side, but with the grooves *running adjacent*. As you reach full depth, you will notice 'square holes' appearing as you intersect the first set of cuts (Fig. 8.4).

8 Clean up the mat with a medium to fine abrasive paper, softening the edges slightly and removing any router burrs around the square holes.

9 Apply a coating of linseed or olive oil with a rag (Fig. 8.5).

Fig. 8.5. Applying a coat of oil to finish.

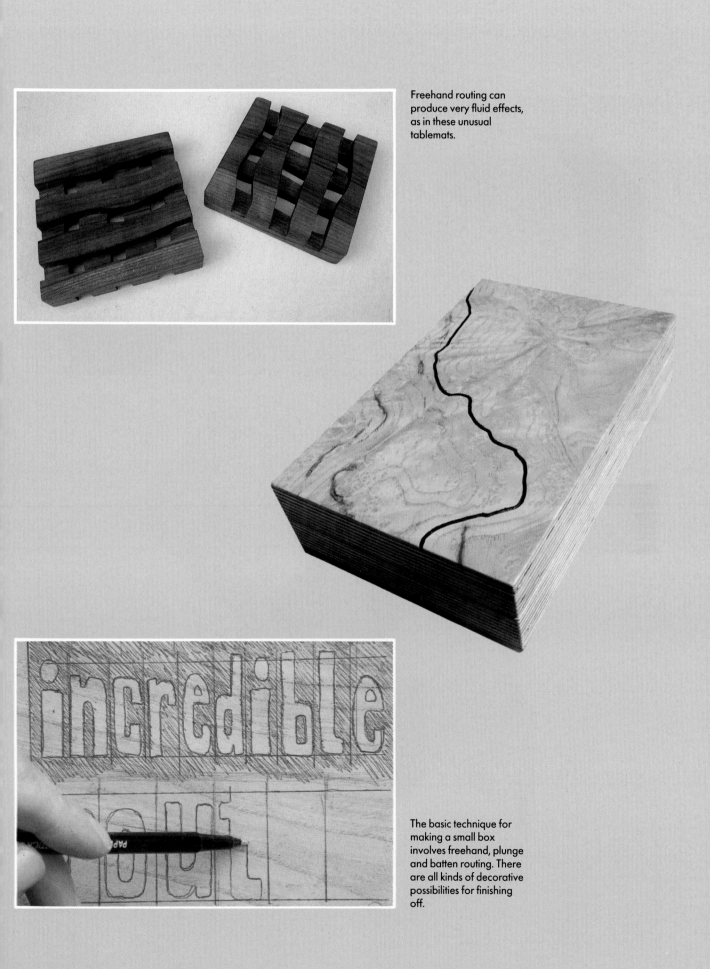

Freehand routing can produce very fluid effects, as in these unusual tablemats.

The basic technique for making a small box involves freehand, plunge and batten routing. There are all kinds of decorative possibilities for finishing off.

Small boxes can be very simple or more complex.

The colourful modern chess set is a good example of the importance of jigmaking in routing.

Attractively grained
lacewood, classically
simple pine, or materials
as underrated as plywood
and acrylic sheet, are
used to make the mirror
base and clocks.

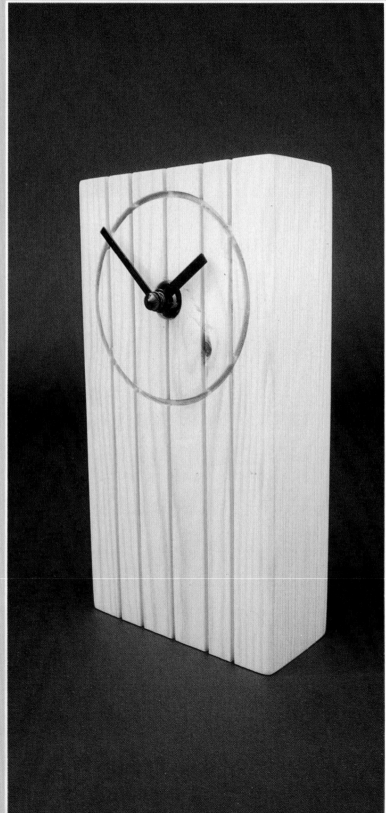

LITTLE BOXES ★

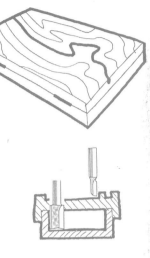

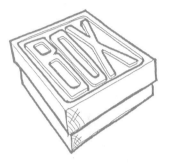

Fig. 9.1. Boxes combine freehand, plunge and batten routing.

Making little boxes (Fig. 9.1) is a speciality of mine; it is a good way of using up interesting offcuts (and usually around Christmas time there is a demand for them). The router is an ideal tool for shaping something slightly different.

These little boxes combine **freehand, plunge** and **batten routing** and the freestyle name relief allows some degree of error if you make the letters bulky (oversize). After all, control of the router comes from trial and error. With experience you can attempt finer detailed freehand routing, as illustrated in one of my veneered boxes where part of the lid features a 1.6mm routed groove which follows the grain.

The router lends itself admirably to the design of these boxes, a departure from the traditional jointed structures. By removing the stock in both base and lid by plunge routing with the fence, an enormous variety of designs is possible in some choice timbers (Fig. 9.2).

Of course this method of using a solid piece of wood to make the entire box does demand well-seasoned stock. I used some

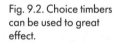

Fig. 9.2. Choice timbers can be used to great effect.

kiln-dried elm offcuts for my design. It is made as follows:

1 Prepare to size the blanks for base and lid. Base: 150mm × 120mm × 30mm. Lid: 160mm × 130mm × 20mm. If you have a disc sander it makes squaring up the edges and end grain that much easier, but if you do it by hand plane make sure that the end

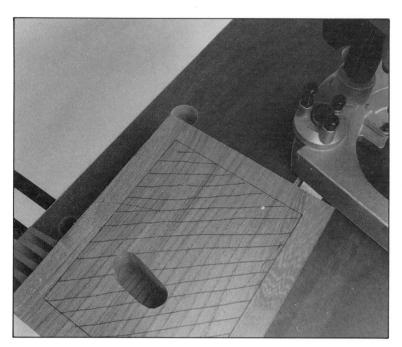

4 After the initial depth-establishing cut, plunge rout in a series of freehand overlapping cuts to remove the bulk of the stock. This is also crucial because the amount of overlap (a crescent-shaped section cut) determines the speed and efficiency of the cut which is plunged straight through to maximum depth each time (Fig. 9.4). I prefer this method of stock removal to horizontal cutting (in stages of depth), as it is quicker and, I suspect, easier on the cutter (and the router bearings). You can see where the chippings go (Fig. 9.5). Work your way from the centre of the box to the wall boundaries and go as near as you dare – let's say 2mm off the line.

5 Fit the fence to the router, align with the wall boundary marked on the wood and methodically trim the inside edge of the wall,

grain is well supported to avoid splitting the fibres.

2 Lightly scribe the 10mm wall thickness around base blank. I used a marking gauge as it is quick, but make sure the scribed line is feint. Now shade waste – the central area which the router will remove. I always shade waste using clear diagonal lines (with a biro) which makes the cut line stand out.

3 Select a 12.7mm diameter straight cutter with bottom cut and fit into the router; secure the base blank firmly on the bench (I use the Black & Decker Workmate with dogs) and start plunging.

The first cut to full depth (25mm) is crucial and this is where instruction is particularly helpful. If you just plunge straight into the wood, you will be sending out smoke signals for another cutter! It will burn. Why? Because there is no escape for the chippings.

On the first cut I vigorously move the router backwards and forwards over a cut of about 30mm long as I simultaneously plunge in stages to the full depth. This creates an escape channel for the chippings (Fig. 9.3).

Fig. 9.3. Create an escape channel for the chippings to prevent smoke signals.

Fig. 9.4. Plunging the cut through a maximum depth each time.

taking off the minutest amount in horizontal passes in staged cuts to the final depth (Fig. 9.6). Care should be taken to prevent the cutter wandering on this operation. It would be easier to set the fence from the opposite side if it is long enough. Also take care in radiusing the corners (Fig. 9.7).

6 It may be necessary to finally skim the entire base surface in order to remove any cutter marks left from the numerous plunging strokes.

7 Using either the fence or a router set in a router table, cut a small rebate all the way round the top edge of the base – 3mm wide × 4mm deep (Fig. 9.8). This is for locating the lid.

8 Mark out the wall boundary on the lid and shade waste (Fig. 9.9).

9 Remove the stock to a depth of 5mm by freehand plunge routing. I prefer to leave a portion of the stock full height in the centre to serve as support for the router, so as to prevent it tipping during plunging (Fig. 9.10). It is removed on the final cuts.

10 Fit the fence to the router and align in order to trim sides of walls, similar to the operation for the base.

11 Use a chisel to radius the inside corner

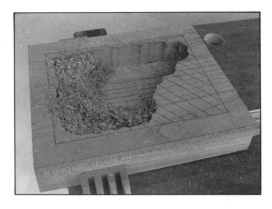

Fig. 9.5. Fast chipping clearance on deep cuts.

lipping of the base to match the radiused routed corner of the inside of the lid (Fig. 9.11).

12 Draw out the design of your lid. To make it easier, block out the letters so that they are evenly spaced and then draw them in, remembering to shade waste. A

Fig. 9.6. Trimming the inside edge of the wall – carefully!

Fig. 9.7. Take care in radiusing the corners.

Fig. 9.8. Cutting a rebate for locating the lid.

in relation to the cutter depth has to be done carefully, so you work from one position and cut away across the stock so that the cutter is in effect cutting an enlarging rebate as much as possible and not a groove (Fig. 9.13).

14 When all the letters have been depicted, work the router out towards the wall boundary line, just short by 1mm or so, then set the fence to the right position and rout the wall line straight all the way round the box lid (Fig. 9.14) to smarten it up.

15 You will no doubt be itching to plane off or sand off the superfluous marks (biro or pencil) in order to see the finished letter-

sufficient gap should be left between the letters for a router cutter to pass easily – say 3mm (Fig. 9.12).

13 Mount the lid on the bench (Black & Decker Workmate with dogs) and rout around the letters, using a 2mm cutter and setting to a depth of 3mm. By tilting the router base I am able to control the depth of cut without the need to keep setting staged depths. Obviously such a deep cut

ing shine through! A final touch could be to stipple the lower surface with flattened-off nails (a bunch held together with masking tape), hammered lightly to give an indented pattern.

16 The final cleaning up is done with fine abrasive paper – as mentioned earlier, I never call it 'sandpaper' because it isn't made from sand! It is either glasspaper, or better still garnet paper or aluminium oxide paper. Soften the edges fractionally with Lubrasil paper or flour paper.

17 Apply some linseed oil with a fine brush (Fig. 9.15).

Fig. 9.10. The router is supported by a full-depth portion of stock in the centre.

Fig. 9.9. Marking out the wall boundary on the lid.

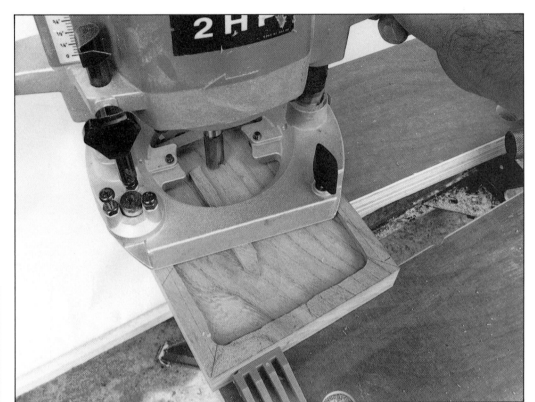

Fig. 9.11. Radius the outside corner lipping of the base with a chisel to match the inside of the lid.

Fig. 9.12. Drawing out the design.

Fig. 9.13. Routing around the letters.

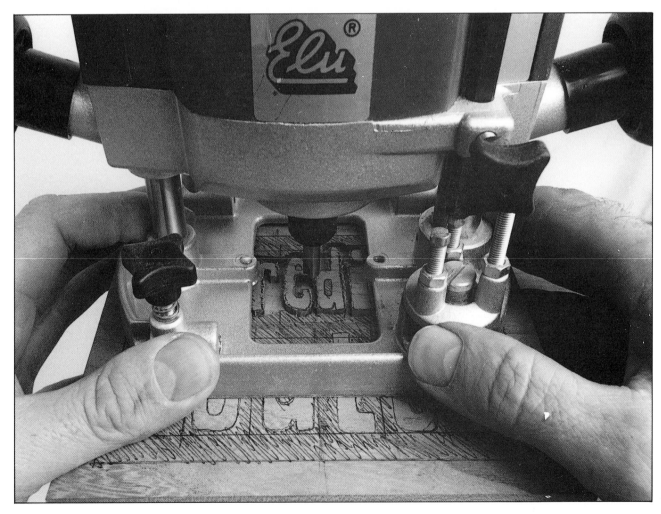

Fig. 9.14. A straight wall line all the way round the box lid smartens the appearance tremendously.

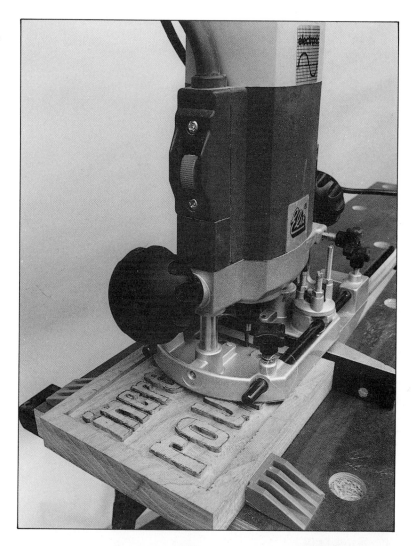

Fig. 9.15. Finish with oil applied with a fine brush.

CHESS SET ★★

Fig. 10.1. The chess set.

Fig. 10.2. Chess board in plywood, grooved for coloured squares.

Modern chess sets are usually distracting from a player's point of view. They may look interesting, but quite often confuse the serious player because the pieces bear no resemblance to the moves. Most serious players prefer the traditional 'Staunton' carved set, myself included, but to make such a set would be quite ambitious and certainly time-consuming.

This chess set (Fig. 10.1) was designed originally for my own use (in 1978) and for a modern set it is relatively 'user friendly'; this is because the symbols graphically express the moves of the pieces, so in fact it would serve quite well for a beginner. It is also quite easy to make, offering various options in choice of materials.

Although my set is rectangular, giving room to store taken pieces, you can of course make a simple square board (Fig. 10.2).

The chess set here is made from 18mm birch plywood with solid sycamore for the pieces. I have used Blackfriars polyurethane stain varnish for the entire set: blue and yellow for the squares and pieces, with red depicting the routed grooves and green for the border of the chess-board! Despite my

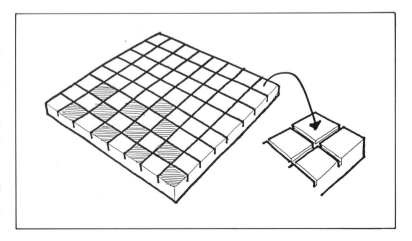

colour blindness, it appears to work quite well. One thing is certain – you would never guess the board is made from plywood (but for the edge)!

The router techniques are really quite straightforward. There is only one cutter employed throughout, and that is a 1.6mm single flute cutter used for **grooving** the board and the pieces. A **fence** is used for the board (plus a **batten** where the central grooves are too far in for the fence to reach) and a simple jig for use with a guide bush for the pieces.

This is a good example of the importance of **jigmaking** in routing. I find it to be almost the most satisfying part of the process – and the part you do not see in the finished item, of course.

As I have said, the routing technique here is fairly straightforward but because you are using the very finest cutter available – moreover one which is extremely fragile – it will demand a very steady hand, a keen eye and a lot of patience. Having said that, the chess set took me only a few hours to make, the board was quicker than I ex-

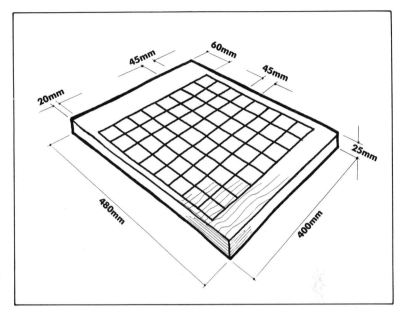

Fig. 10.3. Dimensions of the chess board.

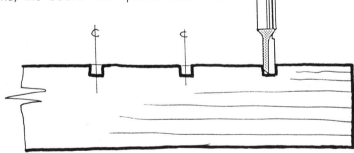

pected, but then one fence setting routs both sides, so you are only setting up for half the board.

The depth of groove is 2.5mm, which is achieved in two passes, and I ran the router in both directions to obtain a clean cut. The depth of cut being greater than the cutter diameter poses a problem if you try to make just one depth cut. Bear in mind that little piece of high-speed steel is rotating at 20,000 plus rpm. The speed or rate of pass is something you find out for yourself – if

Fig. 10.4. Just one 1.6mm cutter is used to groove the chess board.

you are too slow it burns and breaks . . . and if you are too quick it also breaks! I tend to throw away these little cutters after each job, as they are relatively inexpensive and a lot is expected of them.

The stages of making the chess set are as follows:

1 From a sheet of 25mm birch-faced plywood, select a plug-free and interestingly-figured area 480mm × 400mm and cut carefully with a jigsaw – avoiding tearing the grain by either using a metal cutting blade or a fine-toothed wood blade – but cutting just away from the line. Clean up edge with a smoothing plane – or trim with the router against a batten. Power- or hand-sand the surface slightly.

2 The squares measure 45mm × 45mm and there are borders of 60mm and 20mm respectively (Fig. 10.3).

Lightly mark out (with a biro) the border of the large square (360mm square) and draw on the diagonals. Mark the square positions for setting the router fence (Fig. 10.4). The diagonals are vital for locating the end of each routed groove where it meets the adjacent one.

3 Progressively rout the grooves into the board, setting the fence to the appropriate

Fig. 10.5. Use masking tape to prevent split-out of the fibres.

mark, and make a pass between diagonals. Extreme care should be taken, as any overshoot tends to show up rather prominently. One fence setting will apply to both sides of the board. If the total board was square (rather than oblong, as in this case) then obviously one fence setting would rout four grooved lines. As you progress and the squares begin to form you may find that masking tape is necessary to help prevent any split-out of the fibres where the cutter leaves the wood to go into an adjacent groove (Fig. 10.5). After each grooving operation, remove the masking tape and lightly sand over the burr which has resulted (Fig. 10.6), as this will inhibit the smooth

ride of the router across the next groove. Incidentally, always try to sand with the grain, as any scratch marks tend to show up at lacquering stage.

I found a little surgery was necessary to replace the odd torn fibre, which I did with a fine wood spatula, PVA glue and some masking tape (Fig. 10.7). By stretching the tape as you apply it, a clamping action results. Fantastic stuff, is masking tape!

4 On completion of the grooved board, clean up the inside of the grooves by folding over a small piece of abrasive paper and running it along the groove carefully. Sometimes when routing very narrow grooves the waste chippings clog up in the groove (unless you are using vacuum dust extraction on the router). When this happens, use a nail with a ground chisel point and carefully scoop out the chippings. With Lubrasil paper you can fractionally soften or round off the edge of the grooves – but I do mean fractionally.

5 Clean up the entire board and put it aside, ready for stain lacquering.

6 Prepare to size a length of sycamore or similar close-grained pale hardwood. Make sure it measures exactly 30mm square. (The dimensions of pieces are illustrated in Fig. 10.8). The total length can be around 2m (in more than one length), which amply allows for a few extra pieces.

7 Mark out and cut off the pieces to the required lengths (Fig. 10.9) and letter each

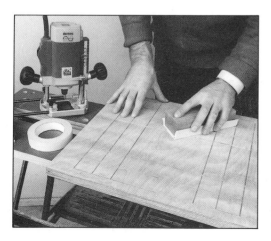

Fig. 10.6. Lightly sand over the burr to allow the router to ride smoothly across the next groove.

Fig. 10.7. Fine surgery using masking tape.

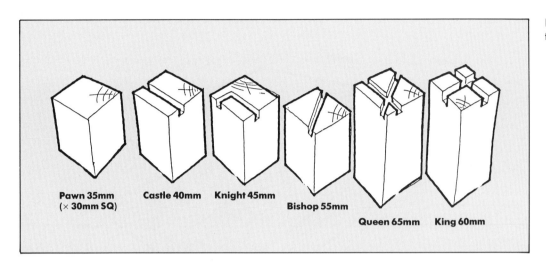

Fig. 10.8. The designs of the chess pieces.

Pawn 35mm (× 30mm SQ) **Castle 40mm** **Knight 45mm** **Bishop 55mm** **Queen 65mm** **King 60mm**

piece on the underside (i.e. K = Knight).

8 Clean up the ends of the pieces, either by hand planing with supporting scrapwood or disc sanding on a table sander. Always work to a line. I use a light biro mark because it is the most effective marked line I can work to (other than a scribed line when extremely fine detail is required). When disc sanding, avoid burning the wood by moving the stock across the disc as you lightly feed it in.

9 Make the jig for grooving the chess pieces (Fig. 10.10). The design is very simple – a plywood base with 30mm-square hole cut in the middle (with a saw-cut to give the hole a tight springiness). A fixing lug is glued in line with one edge of the square hole so that both the chess piece and the jig can be clamped in the vice (Fig. 10.11). An MDF framework is glued to the base and two interchangeable MDF profiled templates are made to fit accurately into the jig. The jig is for guide bush routing – straight cuts and diagonals. You will see

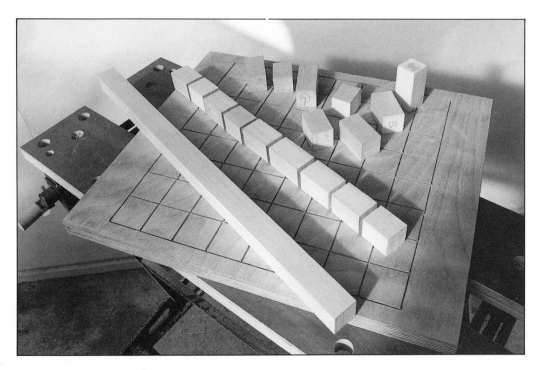

Fig. 10.9. Mark out and cut off the required lengths.

Fig. 10.10. The jig for grooving the chess pieces. Notice how the saw cut gives 'spring-grip' to the pieces.

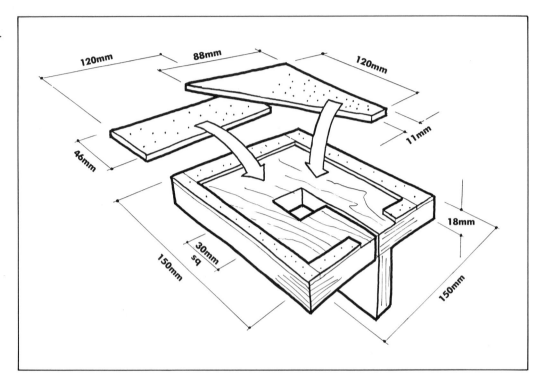

Fig. 10.11. Section showing the chess piece held in the jig with the template inserted ready for grooving.

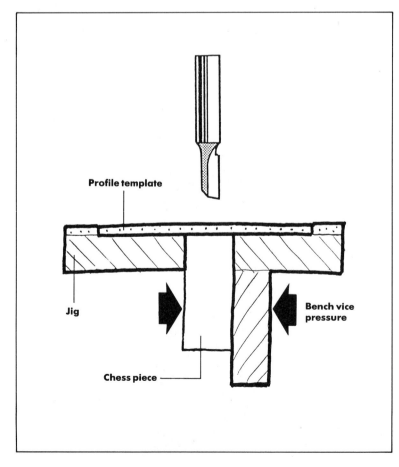

that the design of the chess pieces (Fig. 10.12) relies purely on these two cuts, made either separately or combined, with the templates set universally in the jig as appropriate, without the chess piece having to move once it is clamped into the jig.

10 Insert the chess piece in the jig by lightly tapping it through until it is flush with the base surface (Fig. 10.13). Then clamp both piece and jig into the vice, and insert the appropriate MDF profile template into the jig. I used an Elu MOF 96E router with 12mm guide bush.

Using a 1.6mm cutter, carefully make two or three router passes to cut a groove to a total depth of 2.5mm. The bishop piece, for instance, is a straight through 'diagonal' cut (the grooves intentionally enter the side and not the corner), and is routed in one single operation (Fig. 10.14).

The knight, however, uses the straight MDF template but used in two positions, hence giving the L-shaped cut (Fig. 10.15). A marked line ensures the two grooves meet perfectly.

11 When all pieces have been grooved

84

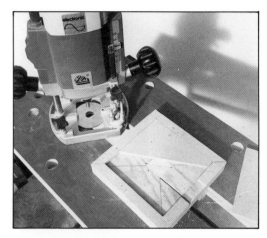

sand with Lubrasil paper after the second coat.

13 With a fine brush apply the red stained lacquer to the inside of the grooves on the board and the pieces (Fig. 10.16). With a rag lightly saturated with turps, wipe away the excess lacquer from the top of the board. If the rag is anything more than *lightly* saturated, excess liquid will run into the grooves, so this operation needs great care (Fig. 10.17). Allow the lacquer to dry for at least four hours.

(the pawns are left plain) clean up the grooves with folded Lubrasil paper and also clean up the sides. I do this by gluing a large sheet of abrasive paper to a board and rubbing the piece against it.

12 Check that both board and pieces are perfectly smooth (all marked lines removed) and ready for lacquering. Brush or vacuum away all fine particles of dust.

The first lacquering operation is to apply two coats of clear polyurethane matt varnish to the pieces and the board. Allow about six hours between coats and lightly

Fig. 10.12. The designs consist of variations of two cuts.

Fig. 10.13. Insert the chess piece in the jig.

Fig. 10.14. The bishop is routed in one single operation (above).

Fig. 10.15. The knight needs the template to be used in two positions.

Fig. 10.16. Apply lacquer to the insides of the grooves on the board and pieces.

Fig. 10.17. Carefully wipe away excess lacquer.

14 With a fine brush, apply two coats of blue and yellow stained polyurethane varnish to the appropriate pieces and squares. Now comes an important point. The white queen always stands to the left of the king, which means that the near left-hand corner square should be dark (Fig. 10.18). This ensures the board is the right way round, and a finer point is to try to get the grain to run in line with your opponent! That's what craftsmanship and design is all about!

15 When lacquering the pieces it is more difficult to avoid runs because of the vertical planes, and the application of stained lacquer has to be done quite swiftly so that brush marks do not occur, so this operation is fairly tricky and loading the correct amount of lacquer on to the brush is crucial. It all comes with about twenty-five years of practice! (Fig. 10.19).

16 The final rubbing-down can be achieved with T-cut or Brasso, just to take the resulting dust particles out of the lacquer.

17 A finishing touch is to line the bases of the pieces and board with felt or baize. Fablon supply a sticky-sided baize in several colours.

Fig. 10.18. Getting the colouring of the squares right.

Fig. 10.19. Lacquering the pieces.

MIRROR ★

Fig. 11.1. The mirror in lacewood.

This project is an introduction to **fence routing**. A small rectangular block of choice hardwood measuring approximately 180mm × 90mm × 30mm is required. I have used London plane or 'lacewood', which has a lovely mottled figure and reflects well in the mirror which is quite simply inserted into an angled groove.

1 Prepare the block to size.

2 Select a single-flute 4.8mm straight cutter and set up in the router to make a groove 8mm deep for the mirror tile. I used a Wolf-craft 'Master Router and Drill Guide' set up with a Bosch POF 500 (500 watt) router (see Fig. 5.9) set at an angle. Using the fence, rout the groove in three or four depths of cut to the lines marked (Fig. 11.2).

3 Select a 6mm radius cutter and rout a series of decorative grooves along the wood. I use the Black & Decker Workmate with dogs to hold the wood, but any method of clamping is suitable provided the fence is free to run along the edge (Fig. 11.3).

4 Clean up with a fine abrasive paper and soften edges fractionally unless a sharp edge is preferred.

5 Apply a little linseed oil.

6 The 150mm-square mirror tile should rest freely inside the angled groove, but a couple of glue-gun lugs could be applied.

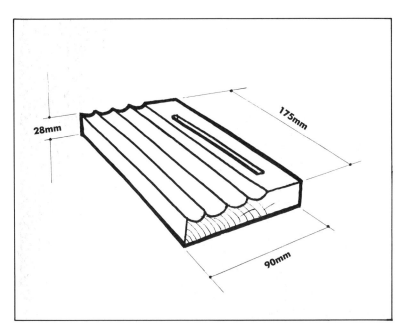

Fig. 11.2. The mirror base.

28mm

175mm

90mm

Fig. 11.3. The fence must be free to run along the edge.

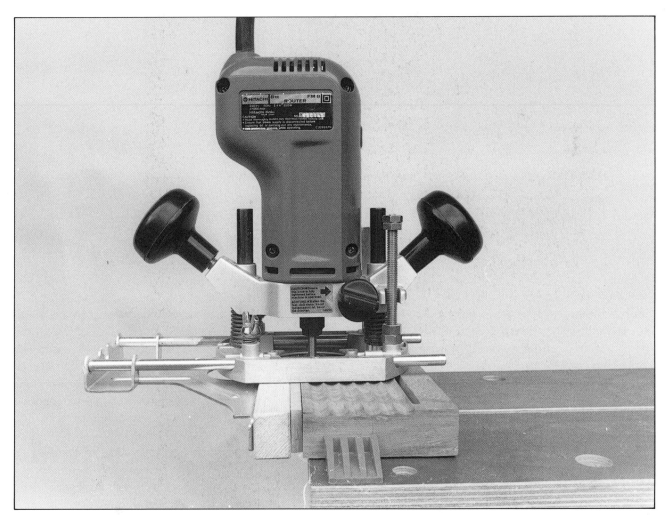

PINE WALL/MANTEL CLOCK★★

Fig. 12.1. The pine wall/mantel clock.

The appeal of a contemporary clock is that the mechanism which allows it to tell the time accurately has been taken care of by the silicon chip, and is the least expensive part of the clock.

I believe there is a perfect blend between the modern technology of quartz battery movements and the router on one hand and the ageless beauty of natural wood on the other, which makes contemporary clocks such fun to design, make and own. As with many of the projects in this book, I designed this (Fig. 12.1) and the next (Fig. 13.1) clock as I went along. The basic challenge is to play around with the function of the time-piece and to explore the use of the router, exploiting the character of the material. By keeping an open mind and throwing all these considerations into the air at the same time, some interesting possibilities can result.

I take much trouble in trimming to size plain rectangular brass hands – which I also spray either black or white, depending on the tone of the clock wood. I seldom use sweep-second hands, but if they are used a protective glass front should be incorporated into the clock-face design. I tend to prefer the simplicity of just two hands. A conical spindle cap can be used to smarten the effect.

Because there are so many possibilities for clocks (see Fig. 13.2), the general purpose of this project is to offer some fairly flexible ideas. I based my designs on the use of the well-proven Junghams 993 quartz movement which measures 63mm square by 15mm deep. You can obtain these with either a long or a short spindle. I chose a long one, hence allowing slightly thicker stock between clock face and movement housing. The clocks can be wall- or mantel-mounted, and obviously the dimensions and choice of materials are fairly arbitrary.

This design can be made from any attractive timber and stands approximately 180mm × 95mm × 43mm. I used pine and contrasted its appearance with black hands. The design is centred around the problem of using the router to depict the digits. By scribing a circle (around which the hands obviously sweep) and plotting the twelve divisions with a compass, grooves are run down the length of the clock face to intersect the circle at these plotted points. The grooves depict all the numbers except for 9 and 3 but as these points are horizontal they are not necessary. A simple idea?

The stages of making this clock are as follows:

1 Prepare clock case to size.
2 Mark out circle and grooves (Fig. 12.2).
3 Set up the router (I used an Elu MOF 96E) with a single-flute 1.6mm straight cutter set to a depth of 2.5mm. Rout the circle either with an MDF female template, using a guide bush, or else trammel rout it to a diameter of 75mm.
4 Attach the fence to the router, set it to the appropriate positions and rout in the longitudinal grooves on the clock face and then carefully along the top edge.
5 Clean up the grooves with Lubrasil paper.

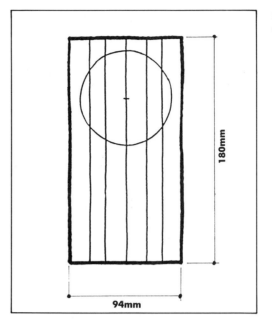

Fig. 12.2. Mark out the circle and grooves.

180mm

94mm

6 Rout a 9mm diameter hole at the centre from the clock-face side, to a depth of 20mm or so for the movement spindle collar.
7 Mark out accurately on the rear side of the clock the position of the square cut-out for the clock movement, using the centre line as a guide.
8 Set up the router with a 12.7mm diameter straight cutter with bottom cut set to depth and remove the stock, freehand plunging to get out most of the wood, then using the fence to trim the edges of the cut-out portion.
9 Check that the movement fits and that there is space for the timber to shrink and hence avoid compressing it (2 or 3mm).
10 Clean up clock case with Lubrasil paper, including the grooves.
11 Lacquer with either stain or clear polyurethane varnish, using a brush and rubbing down in between coats.
12 Cut brass hands to size. I trim them on the sander after cutting with precision pincers or shears. Key up the hands with very fine Wet & Dry paper (dry).
13 Spray hands with black car lacquer, applying thin coats and leaving to dry for twenty-minute intervals. It is best to leave overnight to fully cure before attaching the hands to the movement.

PLYWOOD AND ACRYLIC CLOCK★★

Fig. 13.2. There are many variations to be derived from a basic theme.

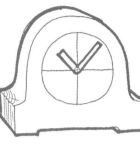

This mantel clock has much appeal and its classic shape combines two interesting materials – Douglas fir plywood and black acrylic sheet . I have been using plywood for furniture making for many years; it is only comparatively recently that it has become a worthy and indeed fashionable material, although its structural merits have been long recognised in the aircraft and building industries.

It is challenging to use a common 'shuttering' ply in a decorative way like this. It is one of my favourites, and you will notice

Fig. 13.1. A classic clock combining Douglas fir and black acrylic sheet.

throughout the book that I use this plywood for both objects and jigs on several occasions.

The clock measures about 150mm high by 150mm wide by 35mm deep, and utilises the Junghams 938 battery-powered quartz movement. It is made as follows:

1 Laminate the sections of 18mm Douglas fir plywood together, using a PVA glue or similar. Make it oversize. Use large G-clamps or sash clamps.

2 Clean up clock case blank surface with

a plane and abrasive paper, using a block. I used a linisher, as it is quick and accurate.

3 Make an MDF template for the clock-case profile and inside trough (Fig. 6.13).

4 Glue-gun a fixing lug on to the underside of the clock-case blank (Fig. 13.3).

5 Attach MDF template to front of clock-case blank, using double-sided tape, and scribe around it (Fig. 13.4). Either cut the external curve on the bandsaw, keeping 3mm away from the template, or use the router with a 12.7mm cutter and 18mm guide bush, and trim the profile in a series of cuts to full depth (Fig. 13.5).

6 Find centre of clock case (Fig. 13.6; I use

Fig. 13.3. Glue-gun a fixing lug.

Fig. 13.4. Scribe around the template.

Fig. 13.5. Trim the profile in a series of cuts to full depth.

The most effective way to achieve a perfectly flat cut is with a router table; in this case I used the Elu Router Accessory Kit table (Fig. 13.10), but you could use the JKB Universal Router table. A 12.7mm diameter straight cutter is used.

9 Draw out the black acrylic fascia using compasses set to the finished recess diameter (not the MDF template diameter), carefully cut on the bandsaw and disc sand to the line (Fig. 13.11). Make it longer than needed, as the end will be trimmed in situ (Fig. 13.12).

10 Drill a 9mm hole carefully in the centre of the acrylic fascia, making sure it aligns

a shop-made centre square), and drill a 9mm diameter hole through the entire case. Reverse the clock case and position the clock movement over the hole, so that you mark the outline of the cut-out (Fig. 13.7). Make it larger by 3mm or so.

7 Freehand plunge-rout the movement cavity to a depth of 20mm (Fig. 13.8) and then set the fence to accurately trim the walls of this cut-out (Fig. 13.9). I used a 12.7mm diameter long cutter.

8 Using double-sided tape, attach the MDF profile template to the clock-case face and rout out the shallow recess for the black acrylic fascia panel. The acrylic is 2mm thick and the recess is cut to a depth of 5mm.

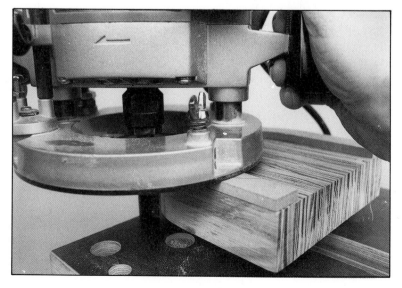

Fig. 13.6. Find the centre of the case (left).

Fig. 13.7. Mark the outline of the cut-out for the movement (right).

Fig. 13.8. Plunge-rout the movement cavity freehand (left).

Fig. 13.9. Trimming the walls of the cut-out (right).

Fig. 13.10. Using a router table to achieve a perfectly flat cut (left).

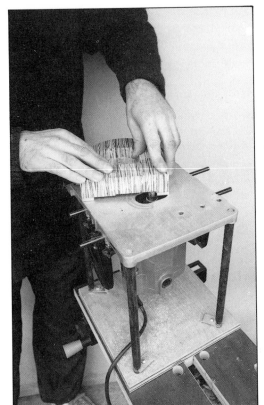

Fig. 13.11. Cut the acrylic fascia on the bandsaw (right).

with the clock-case hole, and marry the two together.

11 The clock is now ready for you to work on the hands; I chose flat brass hands which I trimmed to the exact required size and keyed up ready for spraying, together with the spindle collar and spindle cap (Fig. 13.13).

12 The easiest way to spray the hands is to mount them on the spindle and mask everything off (Fig. 13.14). A series of light spray operations at twenty-minute intervals

– rotating the hands each time to ensure full coverage – does the trick. I used white spray-paint in contrast to the rest of the clock.

13 Clean up the clock case with medium to fine abrasive paper, filling any cavities which might exist in this shuttering plywood. Then apply several coats of clear matt polyurethane varnish with a brush, mounting the clock case on three panel pins stuck into the base (Fig. 13.15). Rub down with Lubrasil paper in between coats.

Fig. 13.12. Trimming the end.

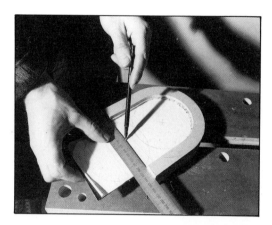

Fig. 13.13. The brass hands, spindle collar and spindle cap ready for spraying.

Fig. 13.14. The easiest way to spray.

Fig. 13.15. Finishing the clock case with polyurethane varnish.

DRAINING RACK★

Fig. 14.1. A simple, effective draining rack.

The draining rack is a simple and attractive idea which blends into most kitchens. Mounted above the kitchen sink drainer, it can be made from a variety of timbers (I have chosen pine). But whatever timber you choose, it must be made waterproof, which can be achieved by brush coating with either yacht varnish or polyester resin.

You can design your own draining rack to suit your particular crockery and cutlery requirements, and you can inset a plastic container to hold assortments of cutlery as well. There are many options to this simple idea (Fig. 14.2), which employs the straightforward technique of **batten routing**.

The stages of making the draining rack are as follows:

1 Draw out your design requirements, which will dictate the size of your drainer, and then select a suitably figured piece of timber and prepare it to size. In my case I joined two different-sized pieces of deal together, making the drainer in two sections (Fig. 14.3).

2 Work out the lengths and widths of the grooves and the number you require by calculating with your crockery. Try to avoid the problem of 'short grain' between two grooves in line with each other, and make sure the crockery is spaced sufficiently wide apart. Ideally, you need the crockery in your hands while you are working this out.

3 Secure the drainer blank on to the bench. I used a mounting lug so that the blank was raised slightly in the Black & Decker Work-mate, ensuring the cutter did not deface the bench on the through cut (Fig. 14.4). Select a 16mm diameter straight cutter which for wider grooves can be achieved with the fence. Make a series of shallow horizontal passes from each end mark until you have cut through (Fig. 14.6). Go easy on the final cuts, to avoid splitting the grain on the underside of the drainer. Use the fence from whichever side is easiest.

4 For routing the short slots for cutlery, I prefer to pre-drill the holes first (Fig. 14.7) to avoid burning the router cutter, then follow through with the router set with the fence (Fig. 14.8).

5 Join the two pieces together using a waterproof glue (Cascamite, Aerolite, Resin W Waterproof, epoxy etc.) and sash clamps (Fig. 14.9).

6 Radius all the routed edges using a 3.2mm radius combination round over/ovolo set, self-guiding radius cutter, and clean up with medium abrasive paper, including inside the grooves.

7 Apply numerous coats of yacht varnish or three coats of polyester resin, applied with a brush (which can be cleaned with cellulose thinner and then warm soapy water). Rubbing down between coats gives a smooth final finish.

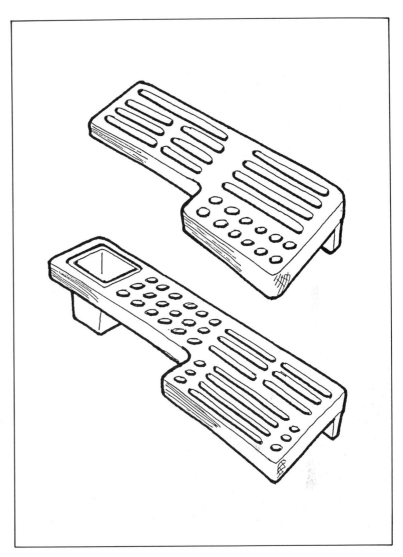

Fig. 14.2. Two design options.

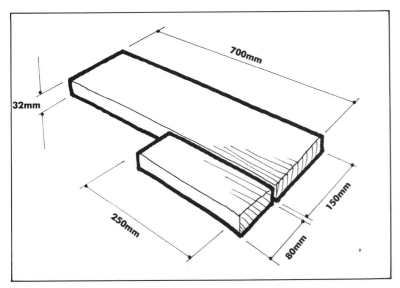

Fig. 14.3. The drainer made from two sections.

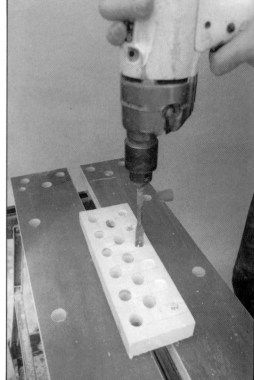

Fig. 14.4. Use a mounting lug to raise the blank slightly (above).

Fig. 14.7. First pre-drill the holes for the short slots.

Fig. 14.5. Section through drainer showing router profiles used.

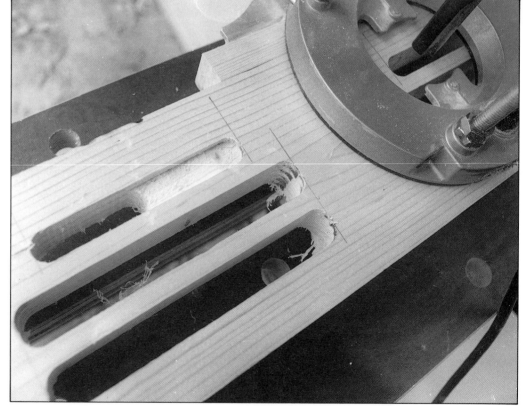

Fig. 14.6. Make a series of shallow horizontal passes until you have cut through.

Fig. 14.8. Follow through with the router set with the fence.

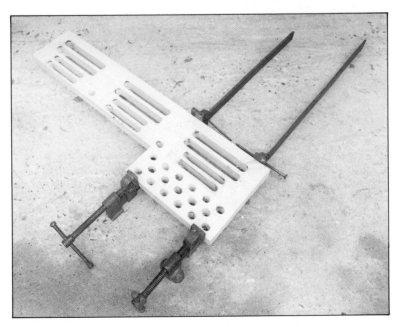

Fig. 14.9. Join the two pieces.

BREADBOARD★

A breadboard or carving dish is an obvious project for the router and this design is intentionally simple and solid in concept, rendering it an attractive and useful household item. The router is capable of adding many **decorative features** if you wish, so this is a basic design to follow or add to (Fig. 15.1).

The choice of timbers should be limited to those which are hard, stable and hygienic to use with foodstuffs. You may wish to consider beech, teak, ash, or even elm or sycamore. The breadboard I made for this project is made from ash and laminated in narrow sections (Fig. 15.2). If you do make joins, it is imperative to use a waterproof

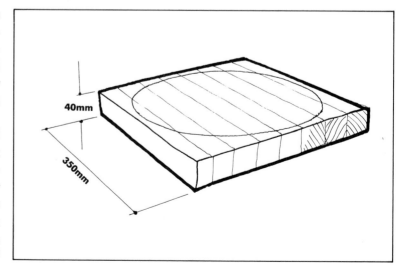

Fig. 15.3. (a) Section through breadboard showing cutter profiles used. (b) Edge profiles.

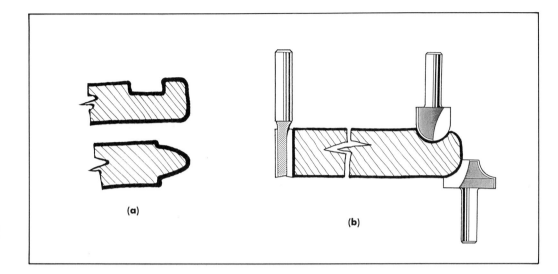

(a)

(b)

Fig. 15.1. The laminated breadboard (opposite, above).

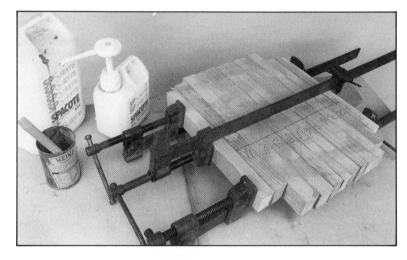

glue; I used a boatbuilding epoxy glue by SP Systems, because the endless washing and drying of a board can open up laminations and harbour bacteria.

The breadboard is made as follows:

1 Select some straight-grained ash from a 32mm-thick board and cut into sections prepared accurately (square) to 40mm × 27mm. The number and length of sections can be approximately drawn out on a scrap board with ruler and compasses.

2 Cut to length oversize of the required diameter (320mm), and set up a dry run in sash clamps. Mix some waterproof glue,

Fig. 15.4. Clamp the glued sections.

Fig. 15.2. Dimensions of the breadboard (opposite, below).

Fig. 15.5. Plane both surfaces.

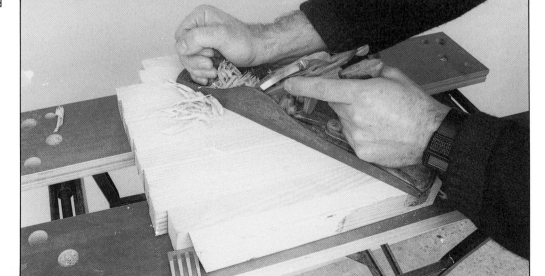

Fig. 15.6. The acrylic sub-base for the router.

the circle (Fig. 15.6). A re-ground stout nail is used as a centre pin and a series of 3mm holes drilled at the pivoting end of the sub-base at intervals for varying circle cuts.

5 Select a long straight-edged cutter, attach sub-base to router and drive pin into centre of breadboard (Fig. 15.6). Set cutter to depth. Glue-gun a mounting lug on to the underside of the breadboard and clamp in the vice, raising it slightly by packing with 6mm MDF (I used a Workmate). Start routing outer circle (Fig. 15.7).

6 Either rout the whole thickness through in a series of shallow cuts with horizontal passes, or remove the apparatus and cut outside the routed line on the bandsaw. Then set up the router and trammel again and trim the final outer curve (Fig. 15.8). I would personally use this method to prolong my router-cutter life. An alternative method to using the sub-base is to use the trammel beam supplied with routers such as the Elu MOF96 which slides through the base.

7 Clean up the edge of the breadboard with abrasive block. I used a linisher as it was much quicker. A table disc sander will do.

8 Set up router with large self-guiding ovolo cutter and radius both edges of the

glue the sections together and set in the clamps (Fig. 15.4). On the 'dry run' I mark a line across the entire laminate structure and number each piece for quick and easy location when gluing. Dry overnight.

3 Remove clamps and plane both surfaces of breadboard blank flush (Fig. 15.5). With a shop-made trammel, scribe the required circumference of the breadboard.

4 Make an acrylic sub-base for the router (I used a Hitachi TR12) for trammel routing

Fig. 15.7. Routing the outer circle.

breadboard, taking care not to burn the wood especially on the denser end-grain (Fig. 15.9).

9 Use abrasive paper to clean up the radiused edges until they are smooth.

10 Rout in the concave lipping around both edges of the breadboard. This operation is best done on a router table with the router mounted below and the board run against a curved or right-angled template. I used the JKB Universal Router table, setting up the Hitachi TR12 router (1300 watts) with a large radius cutter. Set the router to cut in stages to avoid grain breaking and burning (Fig. 15.10). The breadboard should be kept rotating slowly to avoid burn marks caused by the cutter lingering too long. Rout a shallow groove on both sides.

11 Clean up grooves with abrasive paper, working through the grades to obtain a fine finish (Fig. 15.11).

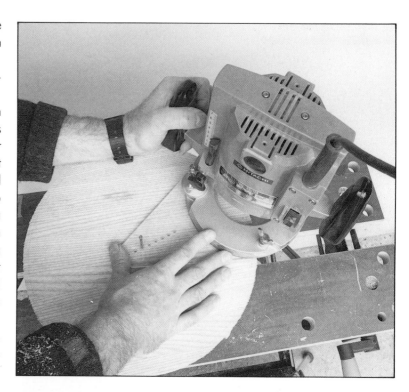

Fig. 15.8. Trim the final outer curve.

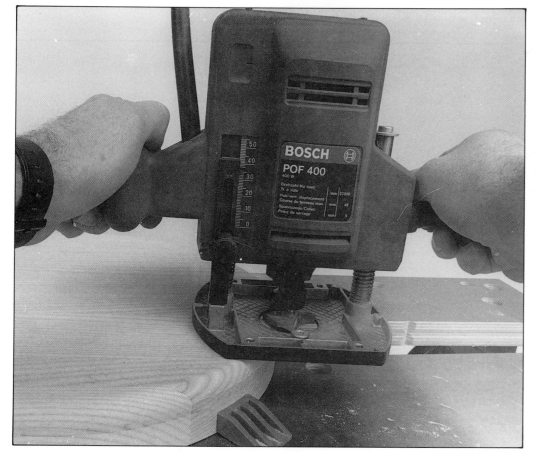

Fig. 15.9. Radius both edges.

Fig. 15.10. Set the router to cut in stages.

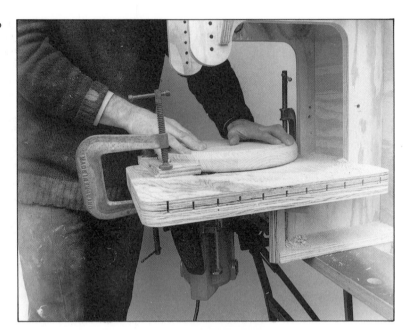

Fig. 15.11. Clean up the grooves to a fine finish.

BOOKENDS★★

Fig. 16.1. Bookends.

I wanted to include in this book the use of a rather unusual router bit – the massive **finger joint cutter** (Fig. 16.2) which I first came across a few years ago. My problem was to design a project around this cutter, which I was determined to use because it is so expressive of router technology and it seems so limiting to restrict it solely to what it was probably designed for – to cut edge joints on boards! In normal applications the joint is seldom seen and therefore not fully appreciated, but structurally it is very strong and gives the advantage of a long glue line.

The Bookends project is also a good opportunity to use some interesting exotic timbers and veneers of which I have a small stock, and to include a 'fake' design which always has popular appeal – although this is a departure from my normal approach to

Fig. 16.2. The finger joint cutter.

designing. In fact, you don't have to own one of these massive finger joint cutters (which needs a huge router to drive it); you can easily make the 'page effect' of the book by using V-cutters or even narrow straight cutters with even the tiniest router. Such is the versatility of routing technology!

While on the subject of versatility, you need not restrict this idea to a pair of book-ends. The concept lends itself to trinket-boxes or caskets, using the same idea but with an opening end cover.

The materials I used were chosen mainly for effect, considering the balance of colour, visual 'texture' and grain etc. The construction is really quite simple (Fig. 16.4); I used Brazilian mahogany for the outer covers and veneered these with burr ash and burr walnut; then I employed a rather unusual South American pine called Loblolly (or *Pinus taeda*) for the 'leaves' and also the narrow supports.

The size of these bookends is approximately 250mm high × 25mm wide × 4mm thick (Fig. 16.5).

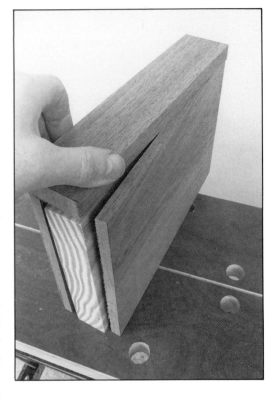

Fig. 16.3. Detail of the finger joint cutter and its profile.

Fig. 16.4. The bookends are structurally simple.

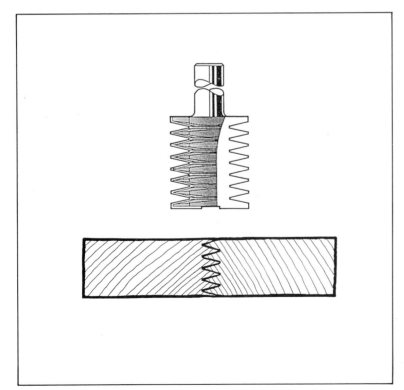

Fig. 16.5. Dimensions of the bookends.

In between coats of varnish, Letraset has been applied to give the bookends a title!

The stages for making the bookends are as follows:

1 Select suitable contrasting timbers and prepare to size (Fig. 16.6). I used a small machine planer thicknesser and finisher.

2 Rout the profile of the pages using the appropriate size router and cutter guiding it with the fence (Fig. 16.7). I used a massive TCT finger joint cutter set up in the Bosch GOF 1700E electronic router. You can achieve the same effect with a much smaller router using V-groove, engraving, or single flute straight cutters, setting the fence each time to run through each cut.

The feature is routed on to the top (Fig. 16.9) and front of the pages blank but not on to the base (which is not seen). If you do use the finger joint cutter, practise on a large offcut first. The depth of cut (or length of finger) is a crucial setting, as the stock against which the guide fence rests can be undercut if the setting is too deep, resulting in an irregular line.

3 Glue the book covers and spine to the pages blank, making sure that the overlap (10mm) is equal on the top and front and that the base is flush. I used masking tape initially to stop the pieces from sliding around once glued (Fig. 16.10) and then carefully placed G-clamps on to tighten the pressure. Clean off excess glue with a damp cloth and fine spatula. Here is a tip for gluing: when spreading the glue on the pages blank, don't go right up to the edge but fall short by approximately 5mm. When the book is clamped up the squeezing glue should not seep out over the edge, and there is plenty of glue contact area left to make it a strong bond.

4 Lightly clean up the book with a smoothing plane and rout the radiused edge (Fig. 16.11) using an ovolo cutter and a fence. Notice how the Black & Decker Workmate dogs effectively grip the work without fouling the fence access.

5 The covers are now ready for veneering. Select some choice veneer for the faces of the covers and perhaps a different veneer

Fig. 16.6. Experiment with visually interesting timbers.

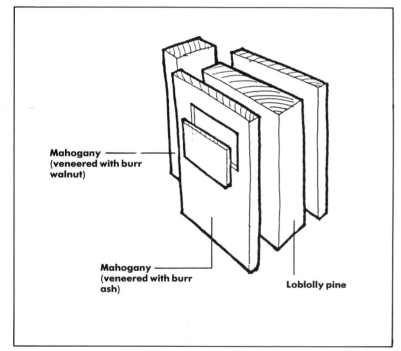

Mahogany (veneered with burr walnut)

Mahogany (veneered with burr ash)

Loblolly pine

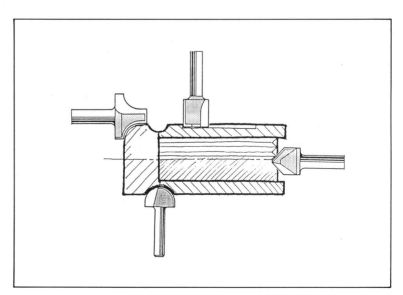

Fig. 16.7. The cutters used for bookends.

for the spine. I used some burr ash and burr walnut respectively, giving an effective contrast. Cut the veneers oversize by about 10mm for trimming when glued. Whenever cutting veneer, always use a backing board (MDF) for the razor-sharp knife-cut to have a firm base (Fig. 16.12).

6 Glue the veneers on to the book spine (Fig. 16.13). I used an Evostik impact adhesive because it is quick and will take the curve of the work without having to resort to special clamping cauls. Apply the glue thinly with a wide spatula and work quickly. I allow about five or six minutes for it to go tacky, then firmly join the two surfaces together. Press the book spine against the backing board to wrap the veneer around in one operation (Fig. 16.14). Don't forget that because you are using an impact glue you cannot slide the work around to align it — you have to locate it on impact, which is why you cut the veneers over size. I use a hammer and scrap block to bed the veneer down firmly. For safety, I placed the veneered book spine into the Black & Decker Workmate and left it clamped for an hour or so.

7 Now trim the veneer carefully with a razor knife, making sure the veneer is supported behind.

Fig. 16.8. Routing the profile of the pages.

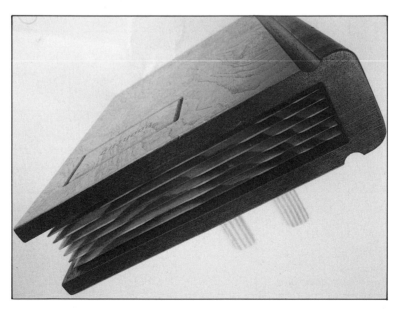

Fig. 16.9. The top of the pages in close-up.

Fig. 16.10. Masking tape stops the covers, spine and pages from sliding around once glued.

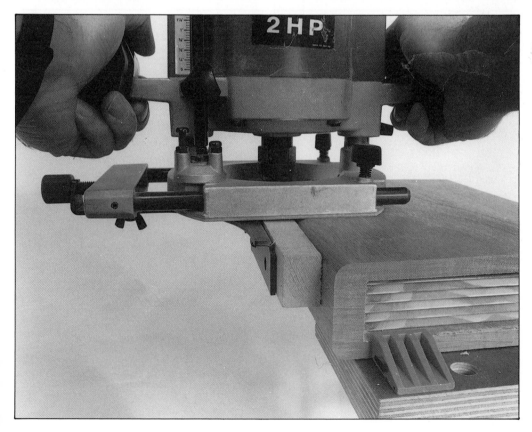

Fig. 16.11. An ovolo cutter and fence are used to rout the radiused edge.

8 Veneer the book covers using the same procedure and ensuring the veneer meets the spine veneer neatly. Use a hammer and block of scrap wood to ensure good contact (Fig. 16.15). Trim the veneered covers afterwards by tilting the book, hence ensuring contact between veneered edge and backing board (Fig. 16.16). You can do this by placing a piece of MDF under the book at the opposite edge.

9 Trim veneered book with sanding block, working carefully into the stock and hence avoiding the splitting of veneer fibres.

10 Set up the router with a large ovolo and rounding over cutter with the fence, and rout a concave groove along the book

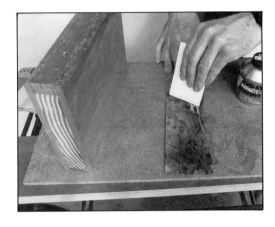

Fig. 16.13. Glue the veneer on to the book spine.

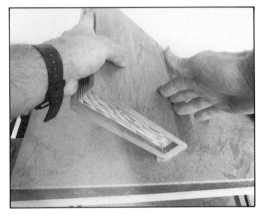

Fig. 16.14. Wrap the veneer around in one operation by pressing the spine against the backing board.

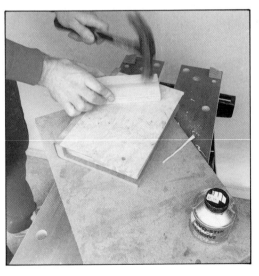

Fig. 16.15. Ensure good contact.

Fig. 16.12. Use a backing board when cutting veneer.

Fig. 16.16. Trim the
veneered covers.

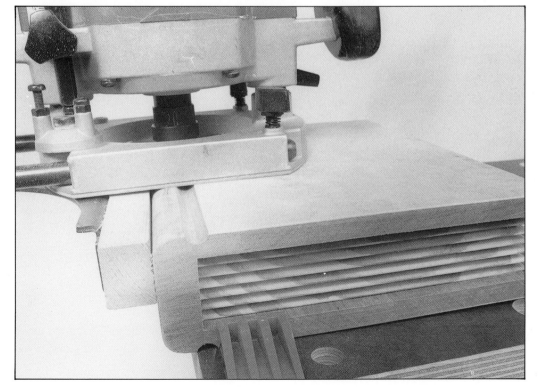

Fig. 16.17. Rout a groove
along the cover where it
meets the spine.

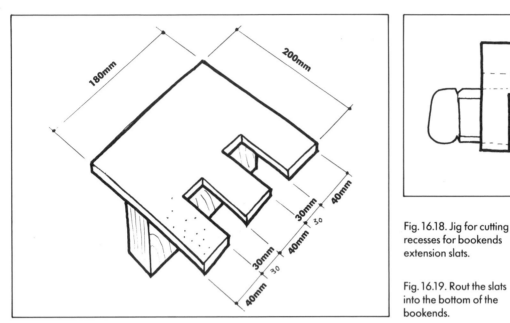

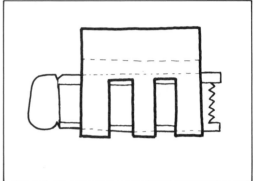

Fig. 16.18. Jig for cutting recesses for bookends extension slats.

Fig. 16.19. Rout the slats into the bottom of the bookends.

Fig. 16.20. Jig in position and stock ready to take router.

cover where it meets the spine (which should also be along the join of the two veneers) (Fig. 16.17). Do this operation in two or three depth cuts to avoid burning.

11 Now clean up the entire book with a medium to fine abrasive paper and soften all edges slightly with Lubrasil paper.

12 Prepare four strips of wood for the stays (240mm × 27mm × 4mm) and make an MDF jig (Fig. 16.18) to rout them into the

14 Rout in a V-grooved border for the title on the front cover if you wish (Fig. 16.22).

15 Use Letraset or similar dry transfer to title the book on the spine and front cover. I applied a couple of coats of varnish first to give it a base.

16 Apply lacquer. I used clear matt polyurethane applied with a brush, the first coat slightly thinned with turps and final applications rubbed down between coats.

Fig. 16.21. The jig and bookend clamped up ready for grooves to be routed in.

bottom of the bookends (Fig. 16.19). When routing in the shallow slots, slide the jig along to a separate position on the second bookend to ensure that the positions of the stays alternate and that the bookends close up on use.

13 Rout in the spine 'ribbings' (actually they are concave) with the same cutter as in stage 10. For this you need a simple right-angle jig (Fig. 16.20). Clamp the jig and bookend into a vice (I use a Workmate) and rout the grooves in (Fig. 16.21).

Fig. 16.22. Routing a V-grooved border on the front cover.

STOOL★★★

Fig. 17.1 (a). The stool/
table in ash.

Here is a project which utilises a completely new joint – the **'rout-kerf joint'**, which can also be applied to a variety of different objects such as cabinet carcasses, nests of tables etc. This is a joint which can be made in narrower section material and used in frameworks as well, so the options are quite numerous (Fig. 17.1(a), (b)).

I first experimented with this joint in its crudest form when I made a prototype sledge a few years ago and tried it out in Glenshie in Scotland. What better test than to risk your life hurtling down a ski slope at an uncontrolled rate of knots on a sledge, using an experimental joint? Well, obviously I lived to tell the tale.

The rout-kerf (Fig. 17.2) has been inspired by the traditional saw-kerf method of bending wood and also by modern loudspeaker cabinet production – 'V-grooving', whereby a V-groove is routed out to all but a fraction of the stock material (chipboard), then adhesive sprayed and the material carefully folded up to make a mitre joint. There is of course no strength in the material at the bottom of the V-groove or the material

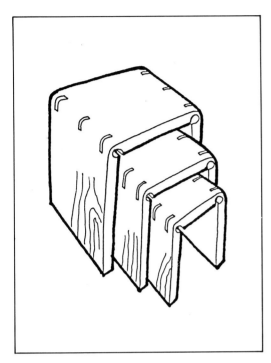

Fig. 17.1 (b). Nest of tables using the rout-kerf joint.

Fig. 17.3. The dimensions of the stool/table.

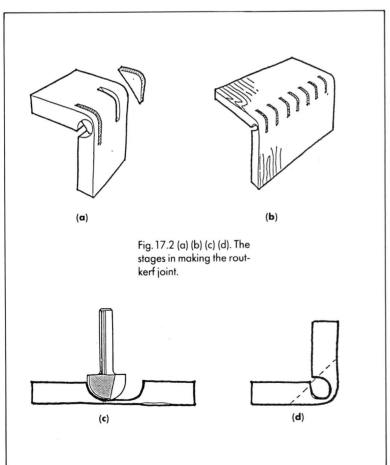

(a)

(b)

Fig. 17.2 (a) (b) (c) (d). The stages in making the rout-kerf joint.

(c)

(d)

in saw-kerfing.

On the sound ecological principle that 'what is taken out should be put back', the strength which has been removed by routing out most of the stock has to be replaced, which is done with another routed-out groove filled with a **solid wood fillet** with the grain running diagonally. Like everything else there is a question of balance in whether or not it works, and in this case the proportions of the sections are the crucial factor.

In order to make the joint, you need a domestic kettle and a board of ash! The stool is really quite simple and in my opinion needs no other decoration or featuring than the aesthetic effect created by this jointing method.

Predictably, the most difficult part is in forming the bend without breaking the fibres of the wood, and the crucial factors (with which I shall deal in detail later) are the saturation of the fibres when steaming and the thickness of stock left after the 'kerf' is routed. Therefore it is quite a difficult joint to make, but with practice on a test piece

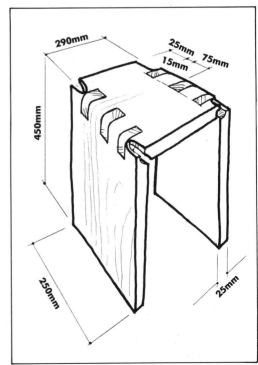

should fall within the capabilities of many craftspeople.

The stages for making the stool (Fig. 17.3) are as follows:

1 Select a well-figured and flat board of seasoned ash and prepare to size – 1200mm × 250mm × 25mm.

2 Mark out the centre lines of the two rout-kerf joints at 450mm from each end (Fig. 17.4), using a large tri-square.

3 Make an MDF jig to rout the rout-kerf joint (Fig. 17.5).

4 Clamp the jig on to the ash board with the marked centre line central and set up the router with a large radius cutter. As such

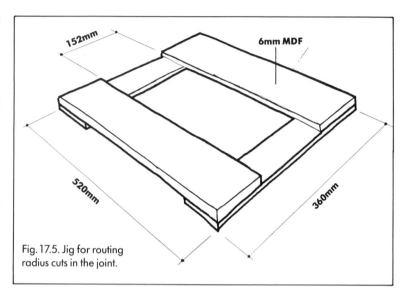

Fig. 17.5. Jig for routing radius cuts in the joint.

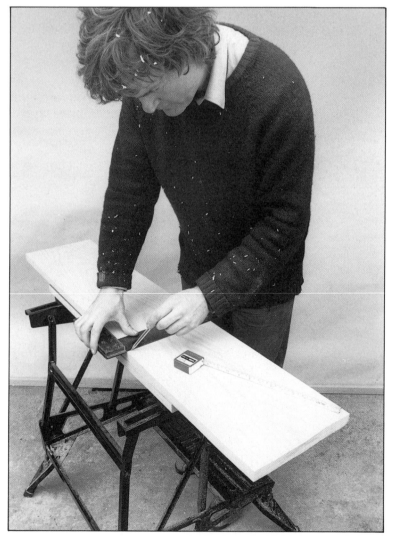

a cutter is expensive (containing a lot of metal) you can use a smaller-radius cutter, but open up the cut more in both depth and width, still adhering to the finished dimensions (Fig. 17.3). Set the depth stop to all but 1.5mm of the stock thickness! (Fig. 17.6). It is vital to thickness the board accurately beforehand, because the only way this method will work is if there is a consistent wall thickness – and that means free of knots as well (which are rare in ash). Carefully rout out the radiused groove in stages, slowing down as you get to the bottom. Notice that the groove is wider than the cutter so that in effect two overlapping grooves are cut (Fig. 17.7). Fine cuts will avoid burns, which are likely because you are routing into predominantly end grain. The routed groove should be clean and consistent and the finished stock thickness between 1.5mm and 2mm, but no more.

5 Repeat the operation for the second rout-kerf joint at the appropriate location mark, and test the joints for 'give'.

6 Now comes the tricky bit, so why not boil a kettle and make yourself a cup of tea while you are at it? You need a kettleful of boiling water to soften the fibres of the ash board at the groove, but I suggest you use a practice piece first in order to get the hang of the technique. This is where two traditions are combined. Normally steam bending demands quite lengthy saturation of the fibres before bending can be achieved. In effect, by pouring boiling water on to both sides of this stock and also directing the steam upwards against the wood (so plug in the kettle and keep it on the boil for a minute or so) we are combining steam and heat bending (Figs. 17.8 and 17.9). I got this technique from my classical guitar-making days, when I used a hot bending tube to form 3mm-thick rosewood for the sides of guitars. A damp rag was used as a liner between wood and bending iron, mainly to stop burning, although obviously

it gave off steam in the process! However, I believe it was heat rather than steam bending. There is no need to be too concerned about the academics of whether this wood bends by steam or heat or both — the point is that it works! You will actually see the wood droop of its own accord but I suggest you support and persuade it by hand (Fig 17.10) until the full right-angle bend has been achieved. This is a very satisfying moment.

7 Carefully remove the wood from the bench (I used a Workmate), place it into the two right-angle jigs (Figs. 17.11 and

Fig. 17.4. Marking out the centre lines of the two rout-kerf joints (opposite).

17.12) which you have already made! — and clamp it firm. It is beginning to look like a stool now. Allow the wood to dry out overnight (Fig. 17.13).

8 Make a jig for routing the reinforcing fingers in to the 'rout-kerf' joint (Fig. 17.14). This jig keeps the stool square and replaces the previous jig, allowing a deep straight cut to be routed diagonally through the timber at various positions across the width of the stool (Fig. 17.15).

9 Mark out the centre line of the positions for the finger joint. I used three fingers; you could perhaps use three or five. The more you have, obviously the thinner they can

Fig. 17.6. The depth stop is set at 1.5mm!

Fig. 17.7. Effectively, two overlapping grooves are cut.

Fig. 17.8. Steam bending, phase I.

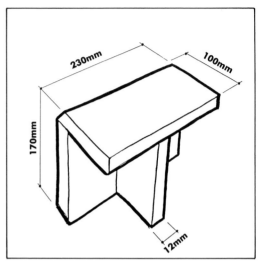

Fig. 17.9. Steam bending, phase II.

Fig. 17.11. Right-angle jig.

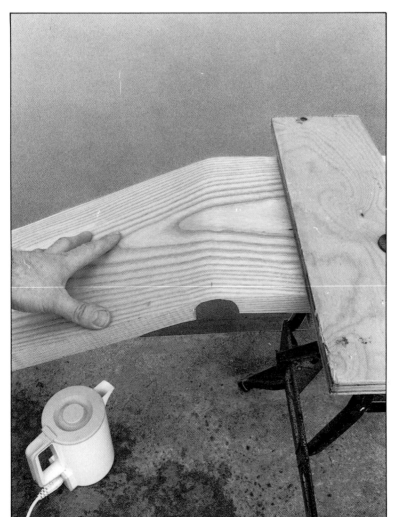

Fig. 17.10. Persuading the wood by hand.

Fig. 17.12. The right-angle jig maintains precision and strength during the routing of the joint.

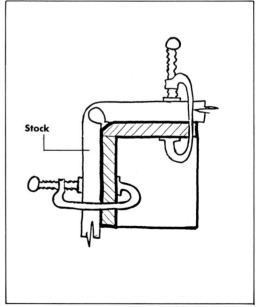

be. Place the jig in position on the first mark and set up the router with a straight cutter. I used a Hitachi TR12 router (1300 watts) and would recommend a similar power rating as the fingers are 15mm thick (12mm cutter) and 36mm deep.

10 Set the router depth stop so that the cutter penetrates 36mm deep from the radiused corner of the wood (this is a little tricky to see, but should be thereabouts). Rout the finger joints in turn, using shallow depth cuts on each, passing the router backwards and forwards within the track of the jig.

11 Remove the jig and replace with the right-angle jig to maintain the rigidity of the stool.

12 Prepare to size a length of contrasting timber for the finger inserts. I used mahogany. Check the thickness by inserting it into a groove until it is planed to the exact thickness required.

13 Insert one end of the mahogany strip

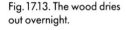

Fig. 17.13. The wood dries out overnight.

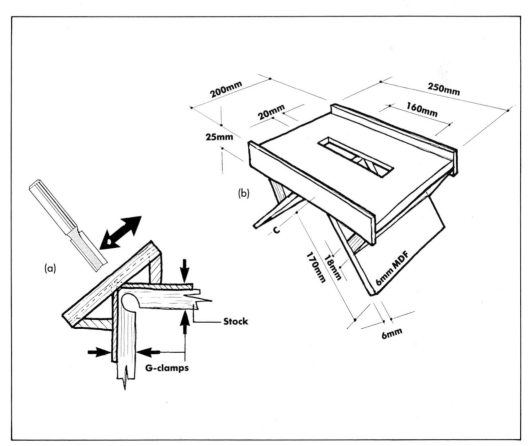

Fig. 17.14. (a) Section through jig showing how right-angle is maintained. (b) The jig for routing reinforcing fingers into the rout-kerf joint.

Fig. 17.15. A deep straight cut can be routed diagonally through the timber at each position (left).

Fig. 17.16. Insert the strip into a groove (right).

Fig. 17.17. Cut off each finger insert (left).

Fig. 17.18. Inside surfaces of joints are coated with glue (right).

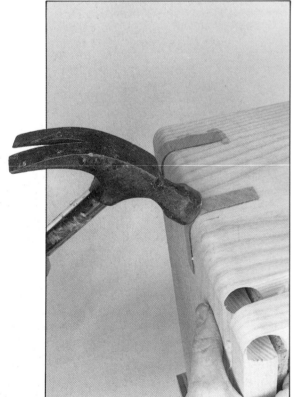

Fig. 17.19. Bed each insert down on the diagonal shoulder (left).

Fig. 17.20. Trim the fingers flush with a simple MDF spacer (right).

Fig. 17.21. Cut away the ash radiused corner to meet the mahogany insert (right).

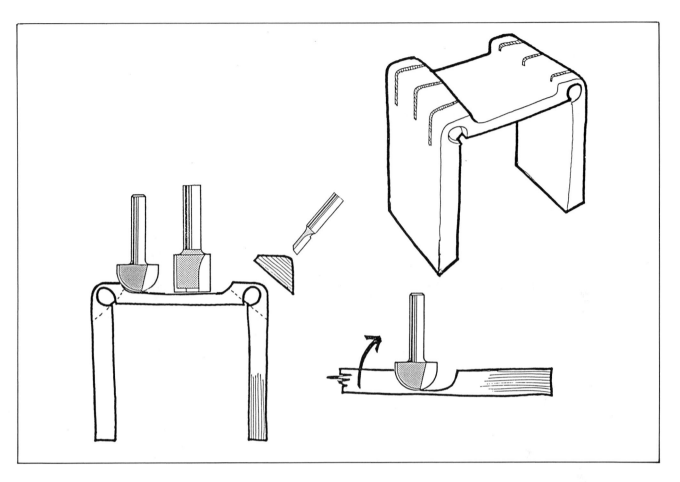

Fig. 17.22. Design options.

into a groove, gently tapping down with a hammer (the fit should not be overtight as it will deform the delicate joint) and trace around it to cut off each finger insert (Figs. 17.16, 17.17). Number the inserts if you like, as each one might need slight adjustment to fit perfectly.

14 With a fine spatula coat the inside surfaces of the joint with glue (PVA or Cascamite) (Fig. 17.18) and carefully drive in each insert with a hammer until they bed down on the diagonal shoulder (Fig. 17.19). Great care should be taken not to deform the joint if the insert is too tight, as the curvature of the radiused stool will be affected.

15 After allowing to dry overnight, trim the fingers flush by mill routing with a simple MDF spacer (Fig. 17.20). Use a straight twin-flute cutter with bottom cut and set cutter depth to fractionally above the stool surface, to leave final cleaning up flush with an abrasive paper block ('fractional' means the thickness of a couple of pages of this book!).

16 The joint is complete except that the edges, being radiused down to 2mm or so, are very brittle and need doctoring. Set the router up with the fence and any 12mm straight cutter, then carefully cut away the ash radiused corner to meet the mahogany insert (Fig. 17.21). Set the fence so that just enough of the thin stock is removed. This beefs up the corner of the stool while retaining as much of the joint detail as possible.

17 Clean up the entire stool with a power sander, working through the abrasive grades, and soften all edges slightly ready for finishing.

18 Apply two or three coats of clear matt polyurethane varnish, rubbing down with Lubrasil paper between final coats.

Figure 17.22 shows a design option derived from the basic stool.

MORRIS NINE MEN GAME★★

Fig. 18.1. Morris Nine Men game.

Morris Nine Men is a simple board game which lies somewhere in between noughts and crosses and draughts. Each player has nine counters which are placed in alternate 'goes' on the three concentric grids. The counters are placed on an 'L', 'T' or 'X' junction.

The aim of the game is to possess all your opponent's pieces, and in order to do this you must make a straight line of three of your own pieces (diagonals do not count as straight lines). You can make a 'three' either by initially placing the counters on the board to make the straight lines, or by moving counters along, one junction at a time, which is the only mode of play once the counters have been placed on the board.

You will not only be attempting to make lines of three but also preventing your opponent from doing so, which means that blocking with counters is an effective weapon of defence. It is therefore a strategy game where the initial placing of counters greatly affects your subsequent mobility around the board. The game is fun to play (no great stretch of the intellect) and is quite easy to make, offering several design and construction options.

You can make the board from any plywood and veneer it if you wish; make the counters from contrasting timbers either circular or square, or make them in plywood as I have done.

The game I have made for this project is made from Douglas fir 'shuttering' ply-

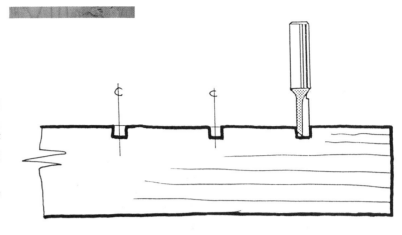

wood with matching counters; the board and pieces have been **resin inlaid** using black-tinted car-body filler! You can of course leave the grooves as they are and not fill them.

The stages of making the Morris Nine Men game are as follows:

1 Select a plug-free piece of well-figured 'good one side' 18mm Douglas fir plywood. If you are making other projects in this book as well, you can buy an 8 by 4 sheet and cut the board from it. Cut the board to size (360mm) and trim the edges square with a smoothing plane. Glue-gun a small mounting lug underneath in the centre of the board for fixing in the B & D Workmate if you have one; or glue the lug near to one edge for fixing in the vice of a woodworker's bench.

2 Using a straight edge and ruler, mark the diagonals on the best side of the board

and also the positions for the three concentric squares (Fig. 18.2). The diagonals serve to indicate the beginning and end of each groove.

3 Set up the router with a fence and 3.2mm single-flute straight cutter, set to a depth of 4mm. I used the Bosch MOF 400 router. The fence only just reaches the inner grid position, so set it to that position ready for routing the grooves.

4 Rout the four grooves to make the inner concentric square, taking care to start and finish exactly on the diagonal line. I find it

Fig. 18.3. A 3.2mm diameter cutter used for grooving.

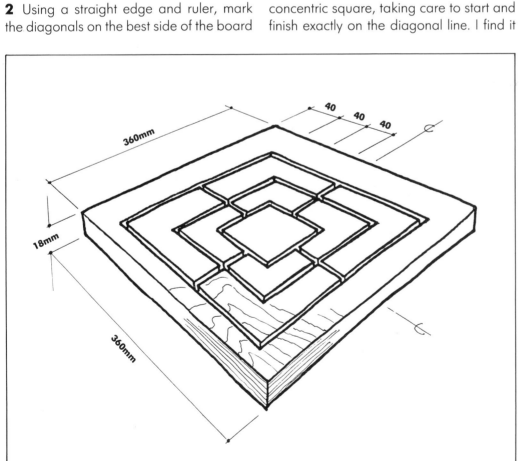

Fig. 18.2. The dimensions of the board.

smaller router bases, don't take this measurement as gospel for your own router as it may be a couple of millimetres out. G-clamp the batten on to the board.

7 Carefully rout the grooves, linking the square grids. Mark the path first with a pencil to avoid routing the wrong bit (Fig. 18.5).

8 Remove the batten and repeat the operation on the adjacent side. This completes the routing operations for the board, unless you wish to bevel the edge with a chamfer cutter. Clean up the surface of the board with an abrasive block to remove burrs from the grooves ready for resin inlaying.

9 Make an accurate 30mm-square MDF

easier to tilt the router base and lower the cutter to full depth rather than plunge each time.

5 Set the fence to the middle grid position and repeat the action, making sure the fence is kept pressed firmly against the side of the board. Then do likewise for the outer grid (Fig. 18.4).

6 Now place a batten across the board at an appropriate distance from marked centre lines to rout the groove to link the grids. Calculate the distance as being from the centre of the cutter to the outside of the router base. The measurement is 60mm for the Bosch I used, and although most manufacturers standardise the section of these

Fig. 18.4. Routing the grooves for the concentric squares (top).

Fig. 18.5. Rout the grooves linking the square grids.

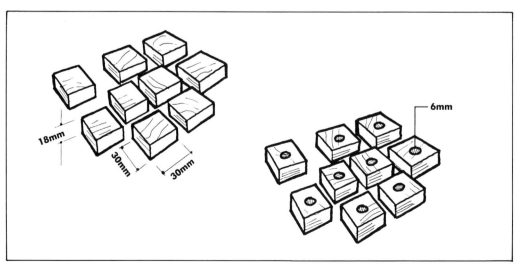

Fig. 18.6. The Morris Nine Men counters.

template for the counters.

10 Mark out the eighteen squares on some 18mm Douglas fir plywood, using the template and leaving a gap of about 3mm between squares.

11 Cut the squares fractionally off the line so that the line is left intact. I used a bandsaw with a fairly fine blade to do this (Fig. 18.7).

12 Sand the counters exactly to the line on a disc sander or linisher (Fig. 18.8), here again leaving the line intact. This is a golden rule in woodworking.

13 Make a jig for router drilling the counters to take the resin inlay (Fig. 18.9). The jig

Fig. 18.7. Use a bandsaw to cut off the squares.

Fig. 18.8. Sanding the counters on the linisher.

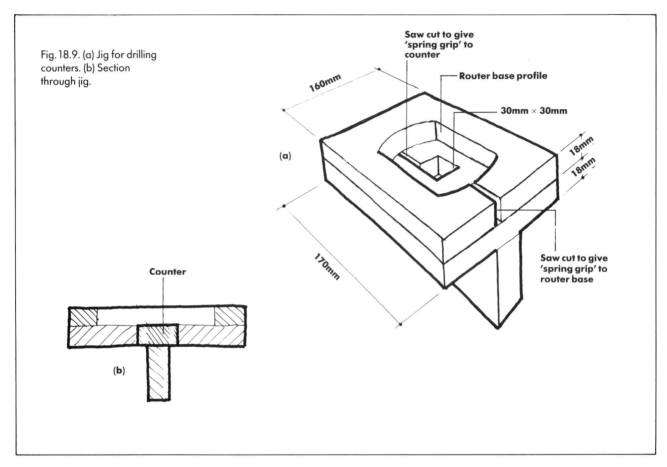

Fig. 18.9. (a) Jig for drilling counters. (b) Section through jig.

Saw cut to give 'spring grip' to counter

Router base profile

30mm × 30mm

160mm

18mm

18mm

(a)

Counter

170mm

Saw cut to give 'spring grip' to router base

(b)

is very simple (as are all my jigs!). Using 18mm plywood, make a base plate with a square hole cut to take the counter. By making the square hole fractionally 'tight' and sawing a cut along the base into the hole, you have a spring grip. Then cut a plywood 'collar' to fit exactly around your router base, again fractionally tight and also with a sawcut. The router cutter should be positioned exactly above the centre of the square hole. I glue-gunned a lug for mounting in the Workmate.

14 Insert a counter into the jig and cover it with masking tape. Using the same grooving cutter set to the same depth (4mm), lower it into the jig and plunge rout the hole (Fig. 18.10).

15 Rout drill nine counters using the jig.

16 Mix up a small quantity of Plastic Padding with some Universal Stainer black pigment (see Fig. 6.17). Then mix 2% hardener

Fig. 18.10. Plunge rout the hole.

and swiftly spread the filler into the counter holes with the plastic spatula provided. It will cure in a couple of minutes. Because it tends to shrink slightly I apply a second fine skim which lies slightly proud, enabling it to be sanded flush with the surface afterwards.

17 Having practised on the counters, you are now ready to resin inlay the board! Mix up small quantities and inlay the board in stages (Fig. 18.11).

18 Allow the resin to cure for half an hour or so and then plane off the surplus with a smoothing plane (Fig. 18.12). If you leave it to cure for days it will be too brittle to plane, because the resin cures in stages rather like

Fig. 18.11. Inlay the board in stages.

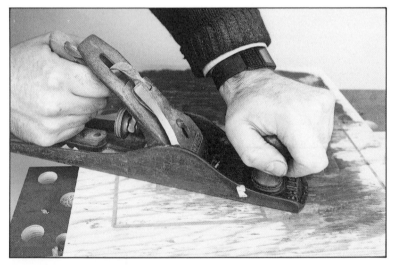

Fig. 18.13. Finishing the board with an abrasive block.

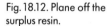

Fig. 18.12. Plane off the surplus resin.

concrete. If you find the sole of your plane is being messed up, then wipe it clean with cellulose thinner, acetate or a chisel.

19 The final stage is a laborious one, and that is to sand down the board (the pieces can be disc sanded) with an abrasive block to achieve a good finish (Fig. 18.13). By fixing the board in the Workmate, I can get a good action going with both hands on the abrasive block.

20 Apply several coats of matt polyurethane clear varnish with a brush to both pieces and board, rubbing down with Lubrasil paper between final coats. Apply some Fablon baize to the base of the pieces and board if you wish.

LAMP★★

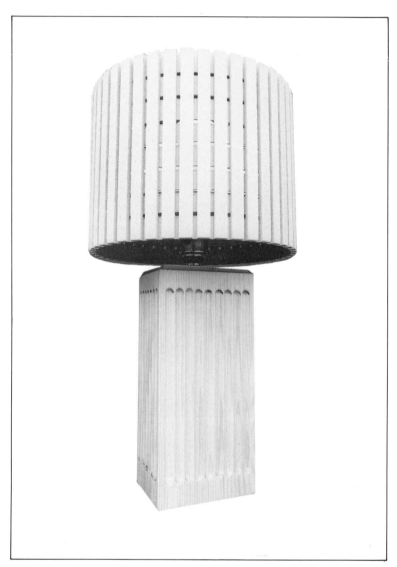

Fig. 19.1. The classic routed lamp.

of the room! This is an attempt to recreate a fairly classic style of lamp while at the same time tailoring it for the router.

The exciting part is the 'shade', which is made of 6mm MDF and is grooved like a **'saw-kerf'** so that it becomes pliable and is then bent and joined up as a circle (Fig. 19.2). The inside of the shade is routed out with similar grooves running adjacently, and like the Table Mat project the grooves intersect and in this case a certain pattern of light is emitted.

It is really quite simple to make, other than a few exacting measurements to make sure the shade joins perfectly. The base is a solid block of wood, glued in two parts, with a groove for flex running down the centre. Any pattern you like can be routed out on the base. A switched brass light fitting is used; this has a flange type fixing to the base, and seats into a plywood disc which forms the shade circle.

You can make this in any size, but I shall set out the stages for making a fairly small one.

Lighting is a very important aspect of interior design. It gives complexion and ambience to the whole environment, and by changing the nature and position of the lighting you can dramatically change a room. For instance, by fixing a light to the wall and shading it you can illuminate that wall and create a soft atmosphere.

However, that is all food for thought and this project is a little more down to earth – a good old English table lamp. I have refrained from designing something too way out, but you could always put it in the corner

Fig. 19.2. Even the shade is routed to make it pliable.

The design of the draining rack is easily adapted to suit different requirements. Batten routing is used in its construction.

Interesting and exotic veneers and timbers were used to make the bookends. The 'finger joint' cutter finds an imaginative application in creating the 'page effect'.

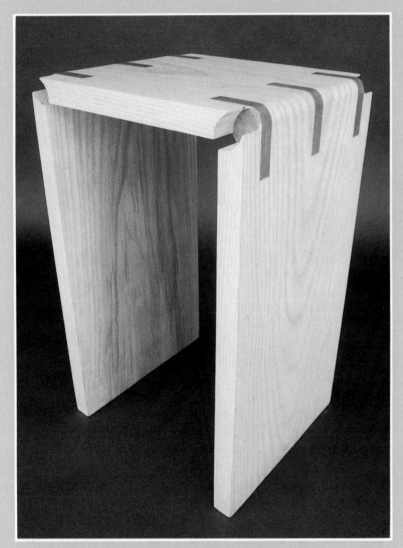

A completely new joint —
the rout-kerf — presents
some interesting
challenges: highly precise
routing, and steam-
bending.

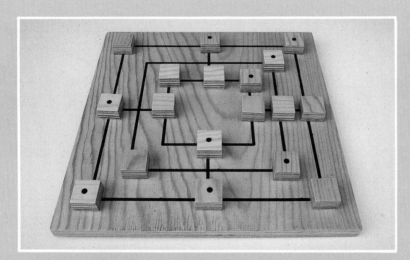

The grooves in the board for the Morris Nine Men game are resin-inlaid.

The lamp's shade is grooved like a saw-kerf so that it becomes pliable.

The coffee table demands
dovetails accurate to
within 0.5mm.

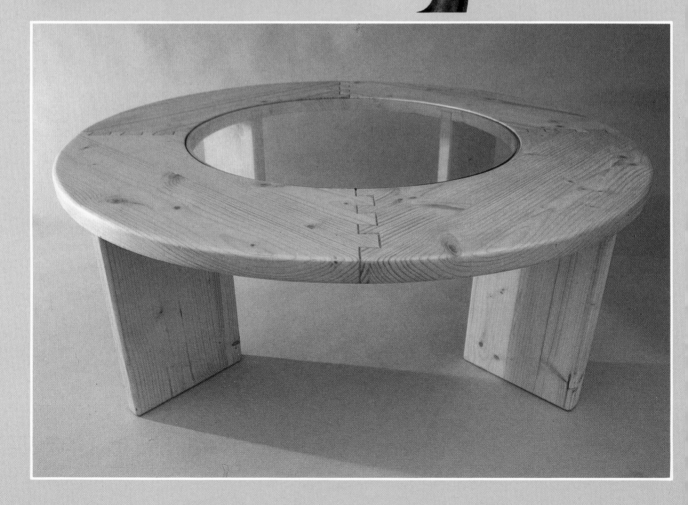

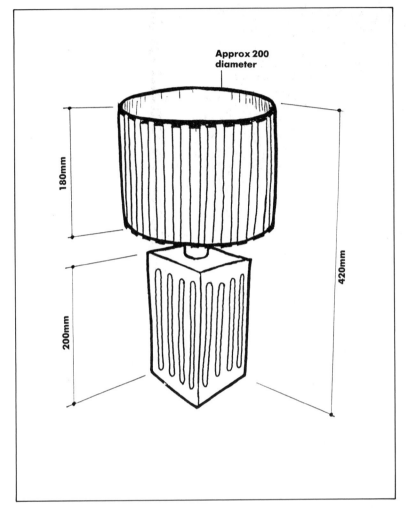

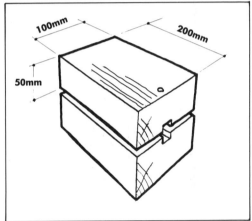

1 Select some suitable timber (any nicely figured wood – I used pine) and prepare to size two matching halves for the base, or leave in one length (Fig. 19.4).

2 Rout a groove along the centre of the base blank for the flex to run through.

3 Cut blank into two halves and glue together, using clamps.

4 Square off the ends accurately. You can plane them by hand or use a large table disc sander.

5 Use the router or a power drill to make the hole for flex near the base, ensuring it joins up with the square hole. It should be about 10mm up from the base.

Fig. 19.3. The dimensions of the lamp.

Fig. 19.4. Prepare the matching halves for the base (above, right).

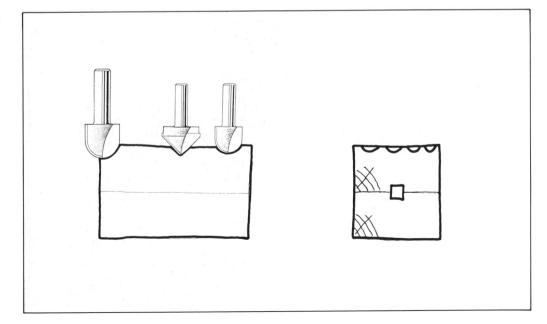

Fig. 19.5. Surface treatment options for the lamp base.

6 Rout the desired features on the sides of the base, by marking out boundary lines. Sketch some ideas on paper first; there are several options open (Fig. 19.5). I decided to employ a fluted look and selected a small radius cutter (Fig. 19.6).

7 Clean up base with medium to fine abrasive paper on a block.

8 Cut 9mm plywood disc to diameter and smooth edge (on a disc sander or by hand).

9 Cut 6mm MDF shade blank to size and check it fits tightly around the circumference of the plywood disc. If you design your own size lamp, use a piece of cotton to accurately work out the required length of the MDF by

Fig. 19.6. Creating a fluted look.

Fig. 19.7. Use a plywood supporting base piece when routing the grooves in the shade.

wrapping it around the disc. Some trial and error is required for final fitting. My shade was fractionally oversize deliberately, so that you can trim either the shade or the disc; the former is easier.

10 Mark out the positions of the equidistant grooves running along the outside of the shade and set up router with a small straight cutter, say 3.2mm diameter. Set and fix a batten to the positions, which should be numbered at each end.

11 Carefully rout grooves on the outside of the shade to a depth leaving about 2mm of stock. The shade is very fragile, so handle with great care. A plywood supporting base piece should be used (Fig. 19.7).

Fig. 19.9. Rout or drill a hole for the lamp-holder to pass through.

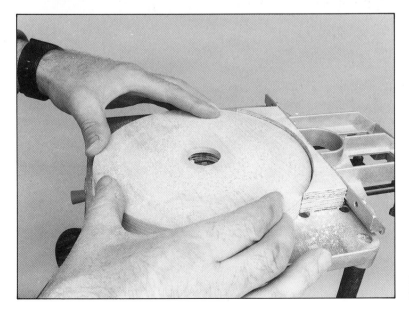

Fig. 19.8. Routing the internal grooves (opposite).

Fig. 19.10. Recess the hole for the lamp-holder.

Fig. 19.11. The shade joint should be perfectly aligned and flush.

Fig. 19.12. Secure the shade to the disc with panel pins.

suit. I used a clear matt polyurethane for the base and left the MDF shade natural for my prototype, but you may wish to spray-lacquer in a colour.

17 Fix the brass lamp-holder on to the base via the flange fitting and fix the shade on to the lamp-holder. Attach the flex to the lamp-holder and feed through to the base.

18 Fix a plug on one end and a 40-watt bulb on the other and switch on! A larger lamp will take a higher-wattage bulb, but keep it to a 60-watt maximum for safety reasons. (Lamps do occasionally get knocked over by the family dog or cat and could be a fire risk.)

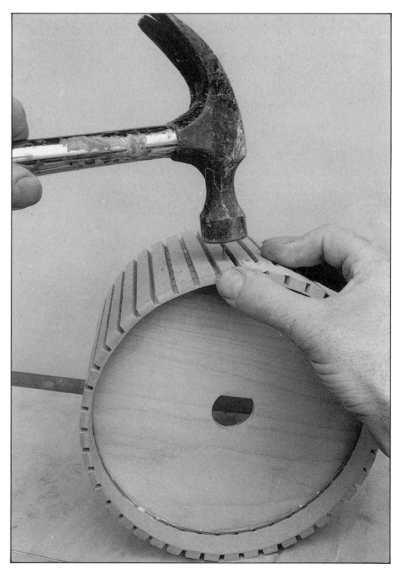

12 Set the router table fence to rout the internal grooves at desired distances and set depth to about half the stock thickness. Where the grooves intersect, a small 'square' hole appears (Fig. 19.8).

13 Rout ventilation holes in plywood disc and also rout a hole for a brass lamp-holder to pass through. This will need to be recessed to fit the brass holder (Figs. 19.9, 19.10).

14 Carefully glue the plywood disc to the lampshade and at the same time glue the join of the shade, using plenty of masking tape. If you have veneer clamps, they are even better. Ensure the shade joint is perfectly aligned and flush (Fig. 19.11) and check the disc is glued in line (use a horizontal groove in the shade as a guide). You may need to use a hammer and fine panel pins to add extra 'clamping pressure' to secure the shade to the disc (Fig. 19.12). If using pins, make sure you sink and fill them.

15 Clean up lamp components with medium to fine abrasive paper.

16 Lacquer the lamp base and shade to

CIRCULAR GLASS-TOPPED COFFEE TABLE★★★

A coffee table is indeed a centre-piece for many living rooms. Even if the majority of the furnishings are mass-produced, an elegant hand-made table can set off the whole interior. A circular table always seems to have a special magic about it; add to that the most recognisable woodworking joint — the dovetail — and you have the recipe for a design of universal appeal.

However, if you are highly skilled and poverty-stricken this project has been designed with you particularly in mind! Putting that another way, you must be able to measure and work to half a millimetre or so, and you probably can't afford a Leigh dovetail jig to produce the intricate 'end-

Fig. 20.1. The circular glass-topped coffee table.

on-end' dovetails in the table-top. In this case you can make a specific **dovetailing jig** for a few pence from MDF to rout the decorative dovetails into the table-top.

If you do have a Leigh jig (Fig. 20.2) then the possibilities of a multi-sectioned top are much greater and easier, but I will deal here with a shop-made jig.

I must admit that I nearly abandoned the project prototype half-way through because of the difficulty in getting the jig sufficiently accurate (four attempts — which I thought readers might find tiresome), and I had misgivings as to whether the four identical table-top segments would fit perfectly together, as any error in angle on the marking out

Fig. 20.2. The Leigh
dovetail jig.

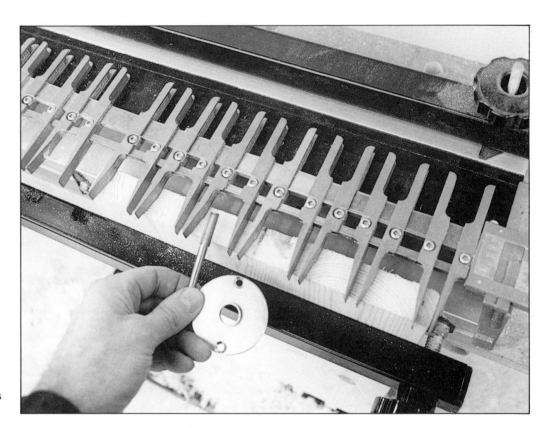

Fig. 20.4. The dimensions
of the table.

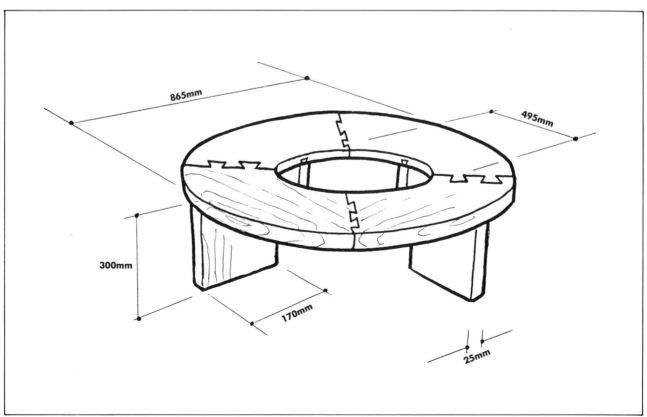

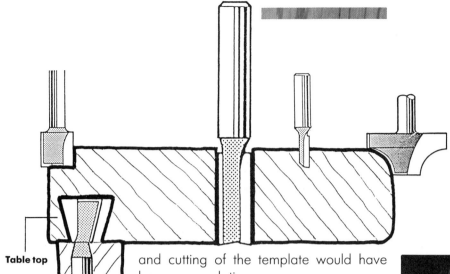

Table top

Leg

Fig. 20.3. Section showing
the range of cutters used.

Fig. 20.5. Template for
table-top sections.

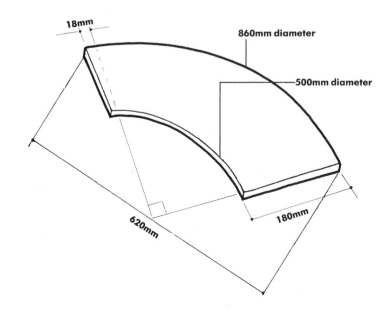

18mm

860mm diameter

500mm diameter

180mm

620mm

Fig. 20.6. Edge-jointing
the table-top material.

and cutting of the template would have
been accumulative.

However, when it came to the moment
of truth it did fit together, though the dovetails themselves were only fairly average.
However, it was an ambitious task achieving
the design in one prototype, so I strongly
recommend you spend time perfecting the
jig first on practice wood, getting the joints
really accurate. This might mean making
the MDF jig several times until it is right and
suits your particular router set-up, but it
serves well to illustrate the tremendous time-
saving advantage of the Leigh jig with its
adjustable fingers.

A fine point worth mentioning – and of
particular relevance to achieving tight router
cut dovetails (whatever the jig) – is that the
clearance between router cutter and guide
template edge is probably not exact all the
way around its circumference; this is

because there is likely to be a fractional
amount of play between guide and mounting rebate, and when screwed tight it can
be fractionally off-centre – and when cutting
dovetails, it is the fractions that count.

One small detail which transforms the
appearance of the dovetailed table-top
(and a feature I use extensively in my own
work) is the **'Danish shoulder'** – a 1.6mm
groove cut about 2mm deep along the joint
line using a simple spacing batten. It's worth
the time it takes to rout out and crisps up
the joint line to perfection! (See also Chapter 7 on Techniques.)

The circular table is 870mm diameter ×
290mm high, with a top 25mm thick (Fig.
20.4). The glass top is 510mm diameter ×
5mm, with a polished edge. The important
factor is the accuracy of the jig for making
the quarter section, as any error will only
multiply fourfold.

My prototype was made of pine (door
linings) 135mm × 32mm edge-jointed to
give double the width. The table would be
even better in timbers such as oak, ash or
elm, but mine was made especially for this

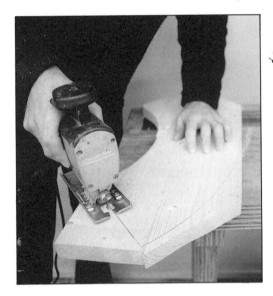

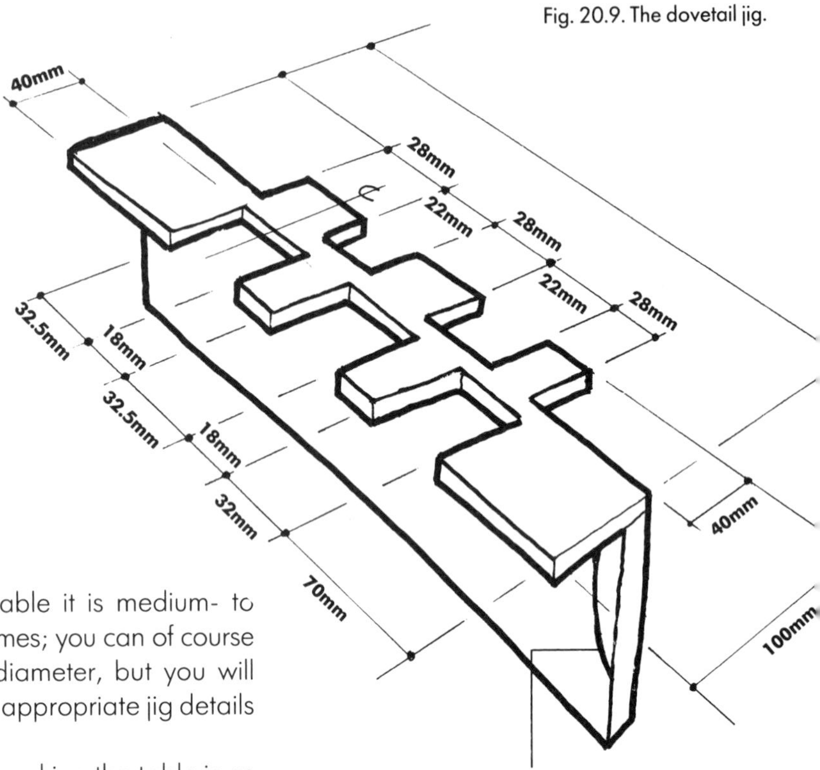

Fig. 20.9. The dovetail jig.

40mm
28mm
22mm
28mm
22mm
28mm
32.5mm
18mm
32.5mm
18mm
32mm
40mm
70mm
100mm

Mark to locate position of stock

Fig. 20.7. Cut slightly oversize round the template.

Fig. 20.8. Edge-trim with the router.

book. As a coffee table it is medium- to large-sized for UK homes; you can of course make it a different diameter, but you will have to work out the appropriate jig details yourself.

The procedure for making the table is as follows:

1 Make table-top sector template from 6mm MDF (Fig. 20.5).
2 Edge-joint table-top material larger than template size (Fig. 20.6). It is unlikely that you will obtain stable timber which is suf-ficiently wide in one piece.
3 Trace around template and cut slightly oversize with a jigsaw or bandsaw (Fig. 20.7).
4 Glue-gun a mounting lug on to the underside of the table-top sector and mount in vice with plenty of clearance for router operation. Attach the MDF template carefully in position on top of wood, using double-sided tape, and edge-trim with the router (Fig. 20.8). I used a long 12.7mm diameter cutter and 18mm guide bush in a 2HP Ryobi router. Make several passes in steps to achieve the full depth of cut. Take care not to break the portion of short grain on this profile.
5 Make dovetail template from 6mm MDF (Fig. 20.9) and test out on scrap wood shaped to the correct profile (curved sides). Remake jig if necessary. This stage is probably the most difficult, but worth persevering with in order to get right. Trial and error is

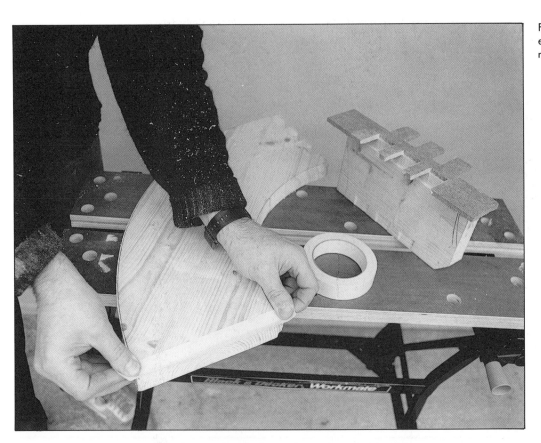

Fig. 20.10. Protect grain
ends of timber with
masking tape.

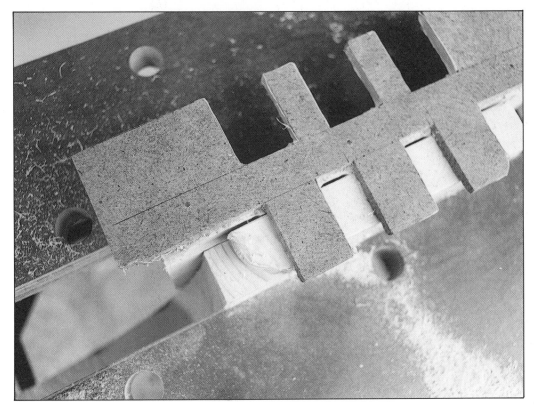

Fig. 20.11. Use both sides
of the jig in turn.

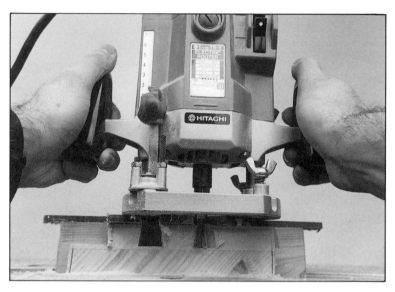

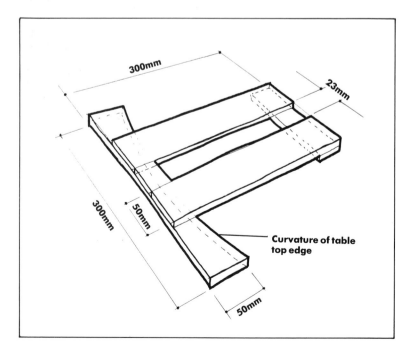

the only way because tolerances on routed dovetails are extremely tight.

6 Set up router with dovetail cutter and 12mm guide bush.

7 Wrap masking tape around the end of timber where dovetails are to be cut to help prevent splitting out of grain (Fig. 20.10). This is quite important, because the grain direction runs diagonally across the dovetail.

8 Mount the timber against the jig up to the position mark and clamp in the vice (the

Fig. 20.12. Feed the cutter gently from right to left.

Fig. 20.13. Easing in the dovetails!

Fig. 20.14. Jig for cutting dovetailed housings for legs.

Workmate is ideal as it clamps wide boards). Cut dovetails and pins using both sides of the jig in turn (Fig. 20.11). Again, take great care not to split the wood because the grain runs diagonally. Feed in the cutter gently from right to left (Fig. 20.12). The best guide is to listen (through your earmuffs) to the sound of the router. You can hear if it is snatching and that usually results in broken fibres.

9 Alternatively, set up the Leigh dovetail jig to cut dovetails, in which case refer to the Leigh instruction manual.

10 Take off the masking tape (apply sur-

gery to any corners knocked off the dovetails) and chisel a 'leading edge' on the underside of the dovetails to ease the fit. Now go and have a quick Scotch whisky!

11 Position the four table-top sectors and gently drive the dovetails home in turn. I really began to wonder whether the fourth joint would line up, as I was aware that any discrepancy in the angle of the template would be multiplied four times. Perhaps I was lucky. Use a hammer and scrap block to ease the dovetails (Fig. 20.13).

12 After the 'dry run' and making whatever adjustments are necessary, glue the joints together and clamp wide battens on either side with newspaper or polythene to prevent glue sticking to them. The point of the battens is to keep the table-top aligned. I use Cascamite glue because it has a longer

300mm

23mm

300mm

50mm

Curvature of table top edge

50mm

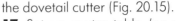

Fig. 20.15. Run through in one pass with the dovetail cutter.

the dovetail cutter (Fig. 20.15).

17 Set up router table (or use portable router with a fence) with the dovetail cutter and rout the dovetail joint on to the table legs (Fig. 20.16). As the joint is a stopped dovetail housing one end is routed out, giving a shoulder-line overlap (Fig. 20.17).

18 Rout a radiused edge on the table-top and the legs (Fig. 20.18).

19 Clean up table-top using plane, spokeshave (if necessary) and abrasive blocks

working period than say, PVA, and is gap filling!

13 Clean up the table-top on both sides with a smoothing plane and true up the circle if necessary.

14 Prepare four legs to size – 280mm × 175mm × 32mm.

15 Make MDF jig for cutting dovetailed housings in table-top (Fig. 20.14).

16 Select a dovetail router cutter and set in router with a 12mm guide bush. Position jig centrally between dovetails on underside of top, G-clamp it, and rout in the dovetailed housings. You may find it easier to start the cuts with a 6mm straight cutter. Lower it in stages, then run through in one pass with

for the edges (Fig. 20.19) and a power sander for the underside (Fig. 20.20).

20 Fit and glue legs into the table-top (Fig. 20.21); I used Cascamite. Check alignment is square and wipe off excess glue with a damp cloth and spatula (or chisel if you are careful). This operation is essential, as glue stains always show up on finished work and it is no good trying to clean off the glue after it has set.

21 Rout the glass rebate into the top, using a straight-edge cutter (Fig. 20.22).

22 Clean up the table with abrasive paper

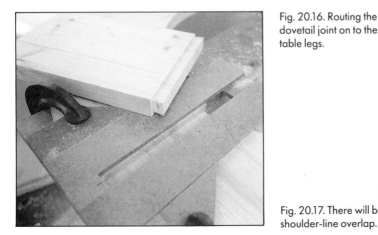

Fig. 20.16. Routing the dovetail joint on to the table legs.

Fig. 20.17. There will be a shoulder-line overlap.

Fig. 20.18. The table-top and legs have a radiused edge.

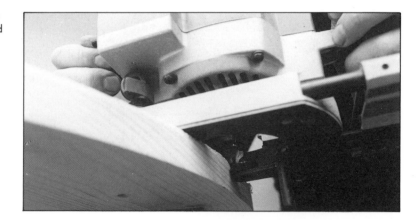

Fig. 20.19. Cleaning up.

Fig. 20.20. Using an orbital sander for the underside.

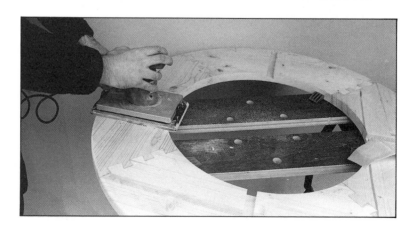

Fig. 20.21. Fit and glue the legs.

Fig. 20.22. Routing the rebate for the glass.

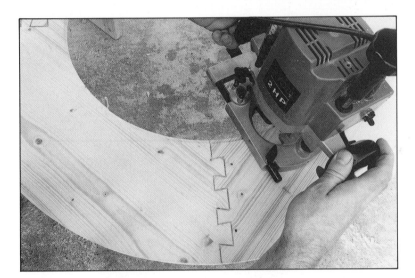

Fig. 20.23. Clean up with an orbital sander.

by hand and with a power sander (Fig. 20.23).

23 Now for the special touch which transforms this table completely! A 'Danish shoulder' is employed along the dovetail joint on the table-top by routing a 1.6mm groove along the glue line. It takes time, but is well worth it (Fig. 20.24).

This is quite simple to do – you make an

Fig. 20.24. Routing the 'Danish shoulder' (right).

Fig. 20.25. Use an MDF spacer to position the batten . . . (centre).

Fig. 20.26. . . . on both the shoulders and tails of the dovetail (bottom).

MDF spacer which is exactly as wide as from the edge of the router base to the centre of the cutter. Use this spacer to position the batten for routing (Fig. 20.25) both along the shoulders of the dovetail and up the tails (Fig. 20.26). Then clamp the battens and rout the groove in carefully to a depth of 2.5mm.

24 Clean up the groove with folded Lubrasil paper and finally sand the entire table, vacuuming away the debris ready for lacquering.

25 Depending on the material you have chosen for the table, you can use a range of finishes. For the pine prototype, I used a clear matt polyurethane varnish applied by brush.

26 The table is now ready for you to order the glass; make sure it is fractionally undersize so as to allow for timber movement.

JKB UNIVERSAL ROUTING TABLE★★

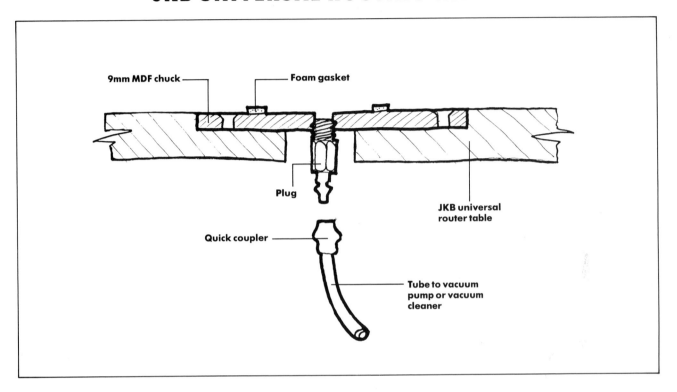

9mm MDF chuck

Foam gasket

Plug

JKB universal router table

Quick coupler

Tube to vacuum pump or vacuum cleaner

Fig. 21.1. Vacuum clamping chuck for the JKB Universal Router Table.

Built for the cost of a few router cutters, this **three-function table** could be the key to your creative routing because of its versatility and enormous potential.

It is designed to serve the following functions:

1 basic overhead routing
2 pendulum routing
3 inverted routing

It can be set up to include pin routing and can be used in conjunction with a vacuum chuck (Fig. 21.1; see page 37–8 for vacuum chuck holding devices). I originally built this table to perform the function of pendulum routing, which is a fascinating routing technique (see Shallow Dish project).

Being made of wood, the table obviously sacrifices some of the rigidity that steel would offer, but that is not to say it is not rigid enough. It is perfectly capable of producing all the projects in this book which require a table-mounted router.

An advantage of wood, as I see it, is that you can easily and freely attach extra jigs,

battens and templates etc. by using pins and the glue gun, and you can also modify the design to your particular requirements. This kind of flexibility is surely the very essence of routing.

Made from a sheet of 18mm Douglas fir plywood and using a portable jigsaw, bandsaw and glue gun to build the prototype, my table has been a useful workhorse right from the start. For your table I would recommend screwing and gluing with Cascamite or PVA, and you can use stiffer plywood (birch or beech) or MDF, but of a thickness no less than 18mm I suggest. I used the glue gun simply to get a working prototype quickly made with the advantage of being able to easily change – beef up, for instance – the ribbings, using this method of gluing because essentially the structure was based on guesswork. Later I had to add the side ribbings/webbings to the lower part of the overhead arm where it meets the stem, as there was some sidewards 'give' in the structure which I had not fully anticipated; at the

(a)

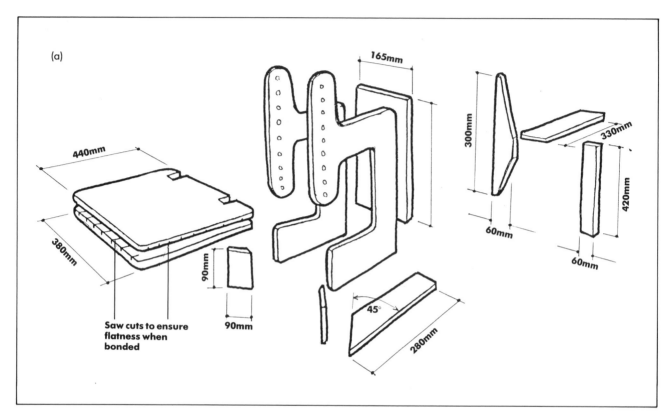

440mm

380mm

Saw cuts to ensure flatness when bonded

90mm

90mm

165mm

300mm

60mm

330mm

420mm

60mm

45°

280mm

(b)

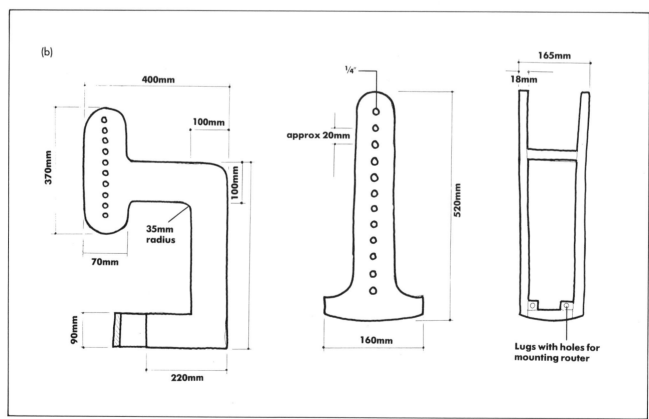

400mm

100mm

370mm

100mm

35mm radius

70mm

90mm

220mm

¼"

approx 20mm

520mm

160mm

165mm

18mm

Lugs with holes for mounting router

144

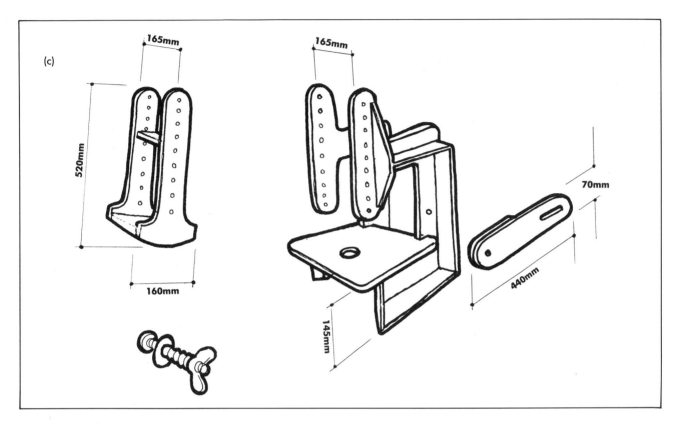

(c)

165mm

165mm

70mm

520mm

160mm

145mm

440mm

Fig. 21.2(c). The router table, arm and cradle, and bar.

Fig. 21.2(a). Exploded, dimensioned view of the JKB Universal Router Table (opposite, above).

Fig. 21.2(b). Dimensions of the basic arm/cradle, and the fixed arm (opposite, below).

same time, I had in the back of my mind the intention of building a basic 'skeleton' which could be easily added to, knowing that modifications or 'fine tuning' would be necessary.

The drawings enabling you to make this universal router table (Fig. 21.2 (a), (b), (c)) give measurements exactly relating to the one I made (shown in the photographs). Before you embark on building your own table, perhaps it would be helpful to give a few specifications of my table so that you can decide beforehand where changes (if any) are to be made.

The table is built to be set up in a Black & Decker Workmate 2. The addition of legs or different lugs can easily change the method of mounting, but the table height in use is 145 mm. It can take any portable router in the inverted position. By using two Trend toggle clamps (Figs. 21.3, 21.4) and recessing the base of your particular router into the underside of the table, a quick release method is achieved. I designed the

recess configuration and toggle clamp positions around the Hitachi TR12 (1300 watts), Ryobi R500 (1500 watts) and the Makita 3600B (1500 watts). When mounting in a Workmate or even on the bench, make sure G-clamps are used – especially at the rear of the table – to ensure it does not come adrift under the weight of large routers being used in the inverted position.

The overhead and pendulum routing facility is all in one. The router sits in the cradle at the base of the arm and either swings from one pivot point (Fig. 21.5), is fixed vertically in the frame with four bolts and wing nuts (Fig. 21.6), or can be angled using the pivots and horizontal bar (Fig. 21.7). The plunging has to come from the router itself. (The JKB Mark 2 model will include a plunging mechanism!)

I specifically designed this arm to take an Elu MOF96E (750 watts) router, but it could also take a Bosch POF 500, Bosch POF 400, Hitachi TR8 (730 watts), Hitachi FM8 (550 watts) and other smaller routers which

Fig. 21.3. Toggle clamps and the recessed base.

Building the router table can be simply achieved by working on the three main sections:

1 the basic stem/cradle assembly (make an MDF template first)

2 the pendulum/fixed head arm

3 the table

Select a good '8 by 4' sheet of 18mm plywood. I always hand-pick all materials as quality can vary. When marking out the various components of the table (and I use a biro as the most efficient marking tool), remember that the grain direction of plywood should be chosen to run in line with the length of each component as far as possible. This is not just an aesthetic consideration; plywood is actually fractionally stronger in one direction than the other because *odd* numbers of veneers are used. (They have to be odd for both face veneers to run in the same grain direction.)

Cut the plywood with a portable jigsaw, using a fine cutting blade to minimise grain

are quite adequate for pendulum and most overhead routing.

Refer to Chapter 7 on Routing Techniques to consider the pros and cons of inverted and overhead routing, and also to the Shallow Dish project for full application of this table.

When not in use, the pendulum arm with its router attached can be swung over the top and rested on the stem (Fig. 21.8), hence allowing quick operation of other functions. In fact, this table is amazingly quick to set up.

You may have noticed that so far I have used the Black & Decker Workmate extensively in this book. It is basically a perfect companion to the router in its tremendous versatility and simplicity of concept (and needs very little advertising from me!). But I have found it to be the most convenient holding device in my small workshop and especially for the projects in this book.

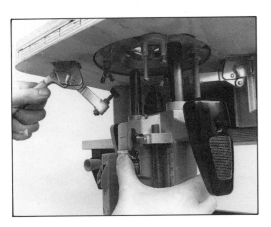

Fig. 21.4. The quick-release method from the underside of the table.

Fig. 21.5. The pendulum arm swings from one pivot point.

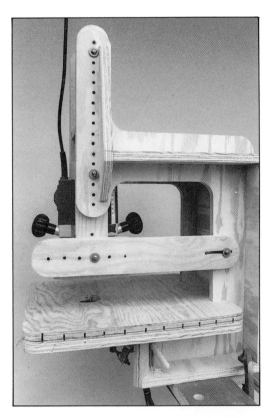

Fig. 21.6. Fixed vertically in the frame with bolts and wing nuts.

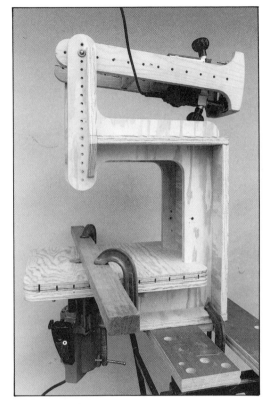

Fig. 21.8. The pendulum arm and router can be swung back out of the way.

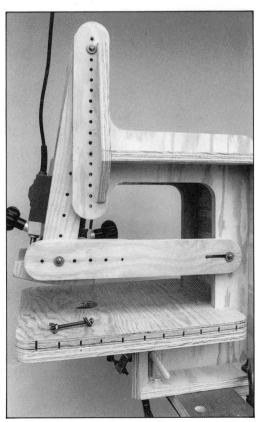

Fig. 21.7. Angled using the pivots and horizontal bar.

splitting. When the pieces are small enough, it is better to use the bandsaw.

An MDF template of the overhead cradle can be made (Fig. 21.2), and then traced on to the plywood and jigsawed out. I used a 12" throat bandsaw for this operation. Clean up all edges by softening with a medium-grade abrasive paper.

Make sure all plywood edges are planed square and are flat, so that firm contact is made at the gluing and screwing stage. I used a disc sander and linisher for cleaning up the radiused sections. All holes are 6mm diameter, drilled with a Black & Decker drill either by hand or mounted in a drillstand. The 6mm bolts used have two stout washers and wing nuts for easy changing.

Building the universal router table is fairly straightforward, and more adventurous readers may wish to develop it further or make it larger. I certainly have plans to build a larger pendulum jig. This table should give a lot of creative mileage to imaginative router users.

SHALLOW DISH★★

Fig. 22.1. Shallow dish made with the pendulum router jig.

This project enables you to design and make a variety of highly attractive shallow bowls and dishes for fruit and other uses. A simple technique of **swinging** a router over a blank of wood from a **fixed pivot point** and scooping out the stock in a series of light **radial cuts** produces some highly effective results, akin to the spirit of adzed woodwork but in a modern idiom.

The pendulum router jig is used to achieve these designs for shallow dishes and platters of a size which it is normally only possible to produce on a fairly large lathe. The con-

cave surface of the dishes can be smooth or fluted depending on the router cutter profile.

This project for a shallow dish in elm is produced on the JKB Universal Router Table, using the pendulum routing facility. On this table it is possible not only to fashion the inside of the dish but to profile the outer edge, also to embellish it with various routed features which I shall describe in fuller detail later on (Fig. 22.2(a)).

Refer to the Universal Router Table project, as you will need to make the table in order to

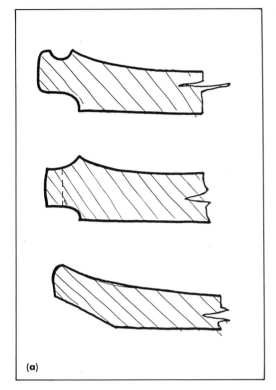

(a)

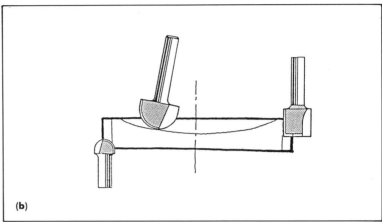

(b)

Fig. 22.2 (b). Section showing the cutter used (above).

Fig. 22.2 (a). Section showing profile options.

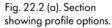

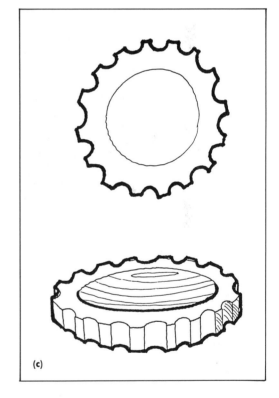

(c)

Fig. 22.2 (c). The design of the shallow dish.

produce these dishes. As I mentioned in that project, the table can be easily made for the price of a sheet of shuttering plywood.

The stages of making a shallow dish are as follows:

1 Cut a suitably figured hardwood blank from a board and prepare it roughly 300–350mm square. It does not necessarily have to be circular as the pendulum jig can profile it later. Plane the base face flat. I used elm as it is well figured, cuts beautifully and can be oiled afterwards. Teak would also be suitable, or even ash or oak.

2 Make a blank mounting jig (Fig. 22.3) and centralise it below the router bit (in its vertical position) and glue-gun it to the table. Glue-gun the disc to the base of the blank (Fig. 22.4). I used melamine-faced chipboard for my jig because hot-melt glue comes off quite easily afterwards without defacing the material.

3 Set the appropriate router cutter in the router. I took off the bulk of the stock with a 12.7mm cutter, then I fashioned a fluted effect, using the small radiused cutter from

the same set. Position the pendulum arm at the correct height setting (I used one hole down from the top). Check clearances and set the router to a fixed depth to take off a 2–3mm cut. My pendulum jig was set up with the Elu MOF 96E router.

4 Start up the router with it held away from the work and swing it firmly and slowly across the stock (Fig. 22.5). To start with, only a small cut in the centre will be made. Make sure the stock material is held firm

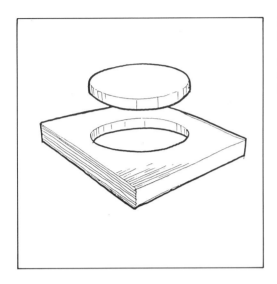

Fig. 22.3. The blank mounting jig.

Fig. 22.4. Glue-gun the disc to the base of the blank.

Fig. 22.5. Swing the router firmly and slowly across the stock.

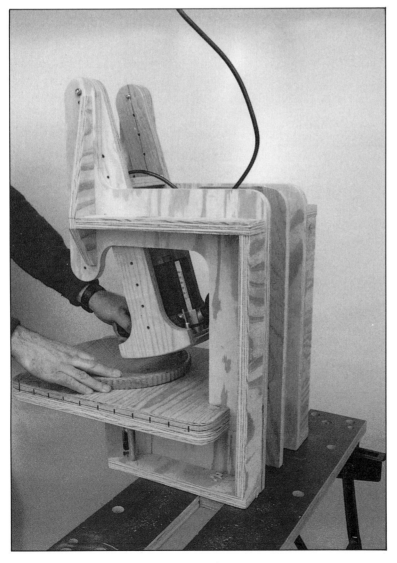

with the other hand. Rotate the work by a degree or two as the router swings clear and then return the swing across the stock for the next cut. Keep doing this in stages until the stock has been rotated a full 360 degrees.

5 Lower the cutter by using the router plunge mechanism and repeat the action, taking a further 2–3mm-deep cut. This operation will be repeated several times until the concave becomes deeper, and to the full width of the stock (Figs. 22.6, 22.7).

6 When the full circumference of the dish has been hollowed out by the flat-bottomed cutter, change to a radiused one and repeat the pendulum action which this time will leave flutings (Fig. 22.8). This operation is more difficult, as you have to judge exactly how much to rotate the dish for each cut and keep it constant. It is a matter of guesswork to get the first and last cut to match up, but if you look ahead a little on the last few cuts it should not be too difficult. A certain irregularity in this method adds to the effect, I feel; and in any case, you can always re-fashion the top by lowering the cutter a few millimetres and starting again. It's all good practice, if tiring on the arm!

7 Now fix the pendulum arm in a set position using a G-clamp; lower the cutter into the stock at its perimeter and rotate the dish so that you work around it forming a circular

Fig. 22.6. The concave becomes deeper . . .

Fig. 22.7. . . . and to the width of the stock.

Fig. 22.8. The pendulum action and the radiused cutter leave flutings.

radiused edge. Immediately you will see that the radial flutings previously routed are now highlighted (Fig. 22.9).

8 Change the router cutter to a narrow straight cutter and with the pendulum arm moved out by about 5mm from the outside of the circular radiused cut, you can now rout the outer edge of the dish. Take shallow cuts and rotate the dish carefully, using both hands on it. Either proceed all the way through the stock or take it out of the jig and trim on the bandsaw, then replace to finally trim with the same cutter.

9 Remove the stock and the female jig from the table (see Fig. 22.4) but leave the jig on the stock. Now you are going to rout in a 'gear cog' feature on the outer edge of the dish. For this you will need to swing the pendulum arm over the top of the table out of the way and use the router (or another router set-up, as I did) to mount on top of the table, with its base plate resting on the dish.

This can be achieved with a series of G-clamps, a spacing batten (the same height above the table surface as the dish) and a fence attached to the router (Fig. 22.10). The female jig is repositioned and clamped to the table with a 12.7mm straight cutter in line with the desired overlap cut.

10 Holding the stock firm in one hand, use the other hand to plunge the router into the dish. A neat half-round cut will result. At this stage, set the depth stop on the router for subsequent cuts.

11 On raising the router cutter from its first cut, then rotate the dish a degree or two for the second cut which should fractionally overlap the first — and so on, until you have profiled the entire perimeter of the dish (Fig. 22.11).

12 Remove all work from the router table, but do not take the circle jig off the underside of the dish as it is needed for the next operation. Mount the router underneath the router table and set up with a 12.5mm radius cutter. This final routing operation on the dish is to feature a radiused lip on the under-

Fig. 22.9. The radial flutings are now highlighted.

Fig. 22.10. Attach a fence to the router.

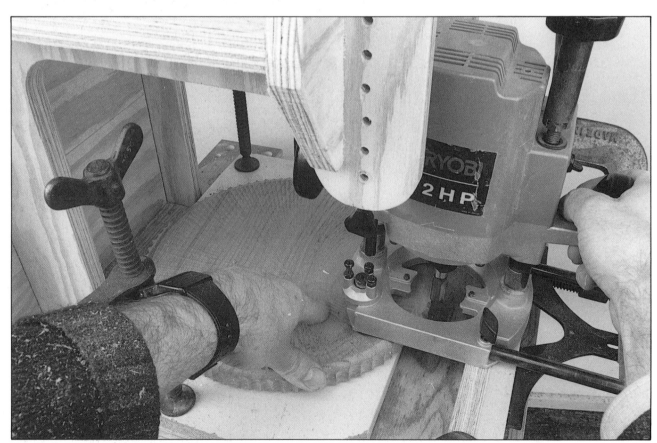

neath. I used the Hitachi TR12 router for this operation, but any medium-sized router will perform the task.

13 Cut a part-circle female jig from MDF or similar material and mount with G-clamps on to the table-top, in a position whereby the dish circle jig (already attached) will rotate freely and present the edge of the dish over the inverted router cutter (Fig. 22.12). When making the part-circle jig, ensure that the profile is less than a half-circle, not more, as a certain amount of backward and forward movement in relation to the feed into the cutter is necessary.

14 Carefully raise the cutter, lock the router plunger and rout the radiused edge profile on the dish by slowly rotating the dish anti-clockwise, so that it feeds against the cutter. Progressively cut the full profile.

15 The routing operations on this dish design are now completed. Remove the circle jig which is glue-gunned to the underside of the dish by prising carefully with a chisel. Clean up the entire dish, and in particular soften the outer edges with Lubrasil paper ready for finishing.

16 Apply linseed or olive oil with a fine brush, working it into the flutings. Attach adhesive baize (Fablon) on the underside of the dish if required.

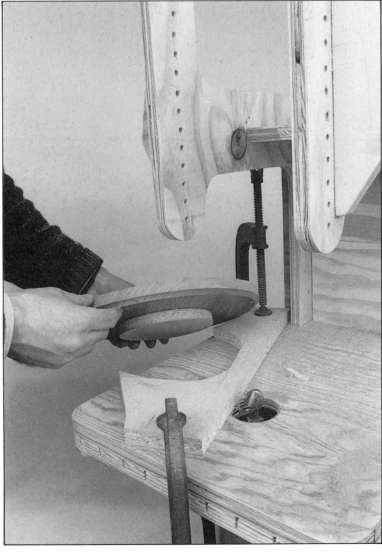

Fig. 22.12. The dish circle jig must rotate freely.

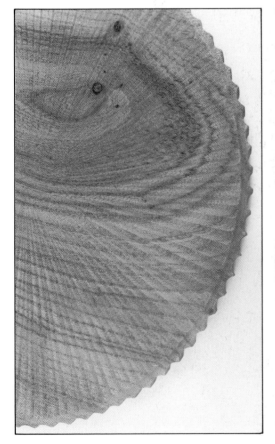

Fig. 22.11. Profile the entire perimeter of the dish.

CHAIR★★★

Fig. 23.1. A chair which combines visual appeal and comfort.

It is written somewhere that if a designer produces a new chair he makes his reputation for a decade, and if that chair is comfortable it is a bonus! This does not say much for chair design generally (or for designers), and despite the countless chairs in existence throughout history only a few happen to meet the fundamental requirement of proper body support.

Chairs are controversial objects. Not only are they special in so far as they are the pieces of furniture we most relate to physically, but in normal use we seldom sit still and in the way for which they were originally

Fig. 23.2. The main dimensions of the chair.

designed on the drawing board, so there are no two people who find the same chair comfortable.

I am not a great believer in the drawing board being the right place to design a chair in any case, but one thing is certain: chairs sell largely on their visual appeal and always evoke interest and debate, so if you want a really comfortable one you should regard chairs like shoes and get one to fit your particular size and shape.

The aim of this project is to give the reader an interesting chair both structurally and visually, which exploits the router and which is fun to make and sit on! What more could you ask for? Oh yes, comfort! Well – build it and judge for yourself!

The chair utilises the Leigh dovetail jig (although it can be made without it) and also my own router joint – the rout-kerf joint. I decided to put the Leigh jig to a fairly stiff test and use the maximum thickness stock which the jig is designed to take (30mm), and attempt a chunky through dovetail.

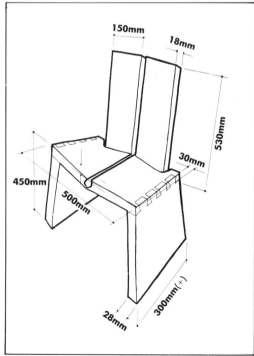

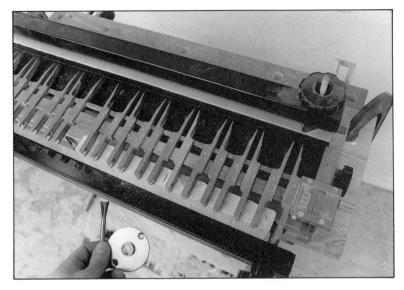

I used 'Rainbow Pineboard' laminated pine, available from Sainsbury's Homebase, which came in two packs measuring 1.8m × 300mm × 28mm (for the seat and legs) and 2.4m × 150mm × 18mm (for the back and under rails). Of course the chair can be made from hardwood and you can prepare your own material to size, but I decided to offer this project with the convenience of buying prepared wide board material 'off the shelf' from the same store where you can buy your router!

If you are going to prepare your own materials, I would suggest one modification to the design and make the seat/leg unit slightly deeper (Fig. 23.2). Alternative materials could be ash, oak or elm, but they should be edge jointed in narrow boards to achieve the required width.

The timber I used (28mm) was slightly under the Leigh maximum. The Trend cutters and appropriate template guides were used and the joints cut like butter. In fact, I was far happier using these large dovetail and straight cutters on a 12mm shank (which incidentally cut in one pass) than the 6mm shank cutters on thinner stock. (Listen to how the router chatters! It tells you all.)

After initial setting up and test-joint cutting, the Leigh jig is remarkably quick and easy to use and I was reluctant to return it to the

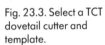
Fig. 23.3. Select a TCT dovetail cutter and template.

Fig. 23.4. Setting the jig to 'all'.

supplier. Imagine making the same journey using a horse and cart for years, then suddenly switching your mode of transport to a Jumbo jet for the same journey? How would it feel?

The stages for making the chair are as follows:

1 From a board of Sainsbury's Homebase Rainbow wood, cut three pieces – two sides and a top to dimensions (Fig. 23.2) – and plane the ends true (flat and square). Cut an additional short length to use as a practice piece for the Leigh dovetail jig.

2 Set up the router with a TCT dovetail cutter with a 20mm guide bush (Fig. 23.3). I used the Hitachi TR12 (1300 watt) router. Mount the wood (the chair legs) into the Leigh jig and set the fingers to the required number and spacings of dovetails. It is advisable to wrap masking tape around the end of the wood first in order to prevent splitting. Set the Leigh jig to the 'all' fitting (Fig. 23.4). Mark the dovetail shoulder line on the wood (thickness of the stock plus 1mm), and set the dovetail cutter to depth with the guide bush in position in the jig.

Fig. 23.5. Cut the bank of through dovetails.

Fig. 23.6. Reverse the finger panel on the jig.

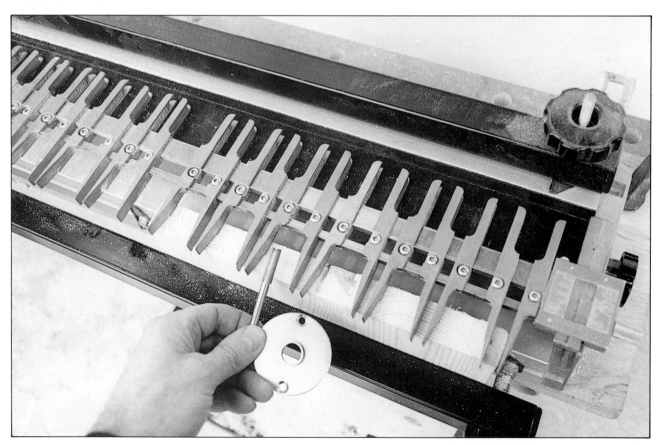

3 Commence cutting the bank of through dovetails in the Leigh jig (Fig. 23.5). You will soon find the router tells you how to approach the stock – from right to left, cutting a shallow curve first to prevent the grain splitting out on the outward motion of the cutter (the right side).

4 Cut the dovetails on the other chair leg.

5 Set up the chair seat in the Leigh jig and change the router cutter to cut the pins – straight cutter. Reverse the finger panel on the jig by sliding it out and flipping it ove from front to back (Fig. 23.6). Set the jig to half a notch below the half-inch setting; that gave me the tightest joint, but check yours on a scrap piece first (Fig. 23.7). Set the cutter to the shoulder line depth. Make sure masking tape is wrapped around the end of the wood.

6 Rout the pins out carefully in the Leigh jig.

7 'Dry' assemble the routed joints using a hammer and scrap wood to persuade them gently home (Fig. 23.8). At this point you can angle the base edge of the chair sides to give the chair seat the necessary rake (Fig. 23.2).

8 Now you are ready to cut the rout-kerf joint which creates a bend in the chair seat (making it more comfortable). Mark a centre line on the chair top from front to back. Set up the router with a hefty radius cutter and G-clamp on a batten so that the cutter passes over the centre mark. Set the depth stop to all but 2mm of the stock. Plunge rout the joint in several steps, taking care not to burn the wood which is mostly end grain (Fig. 23.9). The cut should leave about 2mm of the wood intact, thus giving an easily persuaded 'dry' bend ready for re-inforcement by the cross pieces (Fig. 23.10).

9 Carefully set up the routed seat in a sash clamp and using a steel rule (with zero end mark), tighten the clamp until the chair seat deflects to the 20mm mark at the centre (Fig. 23.11).

10 Make an MDF template for shaping the seat-supporting cross-members (Fig. 23.12),

Fig. 23.7. Half a notch below the half-inch setting.

Fig. 23.8. Persuade the joints gently home.

Fig. 23.9. Plunge rout the joint in several steps (bottom).

Fig. 23.10. An easily persuaded 'dry' bend, ready for reinforcement (opposite, above).

Fig. 23.11. Tighten the clamp until the chair seat deflects to the 20mm mark at the centre (opposite, below).

Fig. 23.12. Template for shaping the seat-supporting cross-members.

Fig. 23.13. Mark round the template.

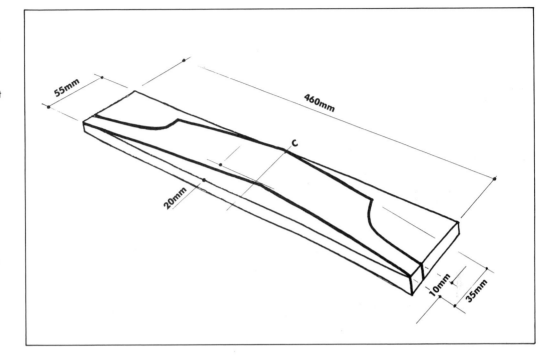

tracing the angle from the clamped-up seat.

11 Select a length of the Sainsbury's Homebase Rainbow Pineboard (from the 2.4m × 150mm × 18mm pack), and mark around the template to cut the three supporting seat members (Fig. 23.13).Cut a few millimetres away from the line. I used a bandsaw.

12 Glue-gun a mounting block under each member and set up in the vice for profile trimming with the router. Use double-sided sticky tape to attach the MDF template (Fig. 23.14).

13 Carefully rout the edge of the cross members using a 12.7mm straight cutter and an 18mm guide bush (Fig. 23.15). Clean up with an abrasive block after removing the glued mounting block.

14 Glue the cross members on to the underside of the seat, making sure all surfaces are cleaned up first. Use G- and sash-clamps (Fig. 23.16) and check that the glue line is tight. I used PVA glue, wiping off excess as usual with a fine spatula and wet rag, and left it overnight.

15 Trim the cross member ends, using the router set up with a stout straight cutter with bottom cut (remove the guide bush), and

freehand rout the ends of the cross members flush with the shoulder line of the dovetail joint! Well, this is supposed to be an advanced project! Now, if the end of the stock is square the routed cross member ends will follow suit, enabling a tight joint to result with a little extra anchorage. Make any final adjustments with a sharp chisel (Fig. 23.17).

16 Dry assemble the seat to the legs and check that everything fits perfectly (Fig. 23.18).

17 Glue the seat/legs assembly together with PVA or Cascamite, wiping excess glue clean from the inside shoulder line. Normally PVA requires about two hours to cure, and Cascamite about eight hours. You will need to cut clamping blocks to allow the dovetails

Fig. 23.14. Attach the MDF template with double-sided sticky tape.

Fig. 23.15. Routing the edge of the cross members.

and pins to extend (Fig. 23.19). Joints are always cut fractionally longer for easy cleaning up afterwards.

18 Trim the dovetails and pins using the router (see the Stool project, page 114).

19 Make an MDF jig for profiling the rear of the seat where it meets the back panels (Fig. 23.20).

20 Mount the jig on to the seat assembly with G-clamps, raising the front edge by a 20mm batten to give the routed cut an angle (Fig. 23.20). Set up the router with a long straight cutter and 18mm guide bush and trim the rear of the seat against the profile of the template (Fig. 23.21).

21 To prolong cutter life you can make a few cuts and then remove the bulk of the wood with a portable jigsaw (Fig. 23.22),

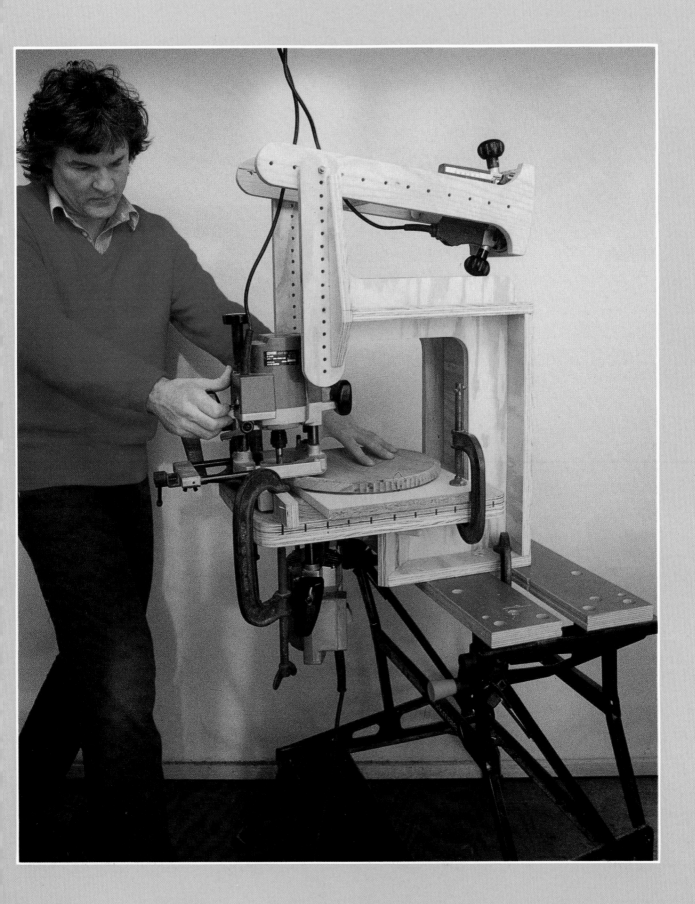

The universal routing table has three important functions: overhead routing, inverted routing, and pendulum routing — as seen here.

A shallow dish in elm is produced by pendulum routing.

Dovetails and the rout-kerf joint are used in the construction of the pine chair. Strengthening fingers are routed in to the underside, linking the back pieces to the seat cross members.

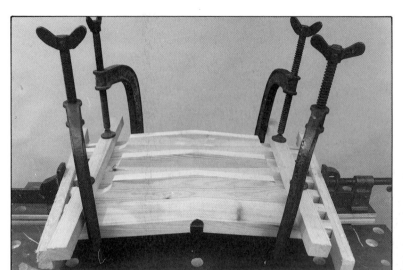

Fig. 23.16. Use G- and sash-clamps, checking that the glue line is tight.

then complete trimming with the router.

22 Drill a hole 60 mm from the bottom end of each back piece and centrally across the width. Screw both back pieces to the rear of the chair with 50mm × No. 10 CSK screws (Fig. 23.23).

23 Using a flat board across the top of the seat and a large try square (I used a roofing square), align both back pieces vertically by pivoting on the screw fixings. The gap between the two panels should be about 25mm and parallel (Fig. 23.24).

24 Now drill two further holes either side of the first one on each panel (scribe a centre line first) and drill a pilot hole through. Remove panels and counterbore all holes

Fig. 23.17. Final adjustments are made with a sharp chisel.

Fig. 23.18. Everything should fit perfectly.

Fig. 23.20. Template for profiling the rear of the seat where it meets the back panels (opposite, above).

Fig. 23.21. Trim the rear of the seat against the profile of the template (opposite, below).

Fig. 23.19. Clamping blocks allow the dovetails and pins to extend.

with the router and then replace, using all screws.

Now comes the interesting part of this chair — the part which is crucial to the strength of the back where it meets the seat, but which you don't actually see. At this point, I recall a conversation I had a few years ago with the furniture maker Alan Peters, who was looking at some of my work for a British event. He said that if you have a technical problem (and that is largely what designing is about) either 'tell the world about it' or conceal it. However, it is easy to get caught in between. By telling the world, you are making a feature out of that problem and many designs achieve just that. There was a problem in designing this chair as I went along, as to how to make the back stronger without destroying its visual simplicity (my main goal in designing). The solution is 'concealed', but it also has in mind that breed of people who — at exhibitions in particular — insist on getting down on their knees and inspecting the underside of a piece of furniture!

The solution is to rout in some strengthening fingers which link the back pieces to the chair seat cross members. It works!

25 Turn the chair upside down on the bench and mark the ends of the back members flush with the angle of the seat cross members. This is easily done by extending a steel rule flat across the cross members and transferring marks on to the inside of the back panels. Allowing for the thickness of the steel rule, scribe a line across and bandsaw the two panel ends. Re-fit and touch up with a small plane if necessary.

26 Glue the back panels in position and tighten the screws to serve as clamps. Leave for two hours if using PVA glue.

27 Cut a small 'slat' of 6mm MDF and glue-gun on to the cross members so that

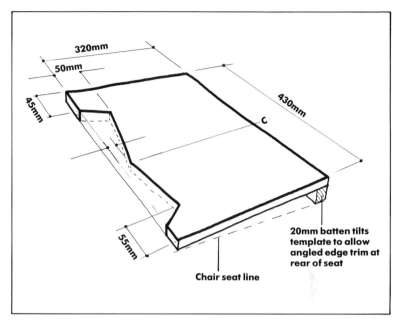

320mm
50mm
45mm
55mm
430mm
C
20mm batten tilts template to allow angled edge trim at rear of seat
Chair seat line

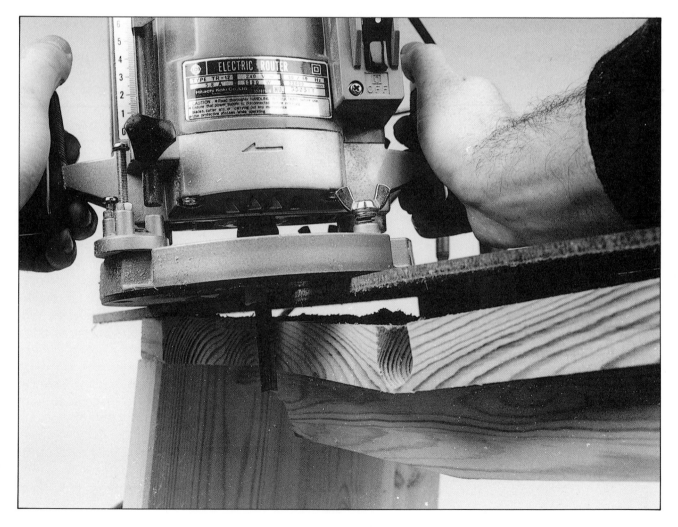

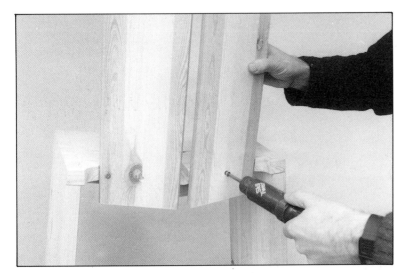

the router which is set up with a 10mm cutter and 18mm guide bush will run a groove in the first position. As this is an advanced project, you can work out the positions of the fingers for yourself (the section of the material is 20mm × 10mm). Rout the first groove in from the middle cross member to the back one, and straight through the chair back (Fig. 23.25).

28 Remove the 'slat' carefully, glue-gun into the next position and repeat the action. Rout all four grooves.

29 Prepare the reinforcing strips from the 18mm Rainbow Pineboard and fit them into the grooves. Make sure they are a tight fit.

30 Glue the reinforcing strips into their grooves, gently tapping them home with a hammer and scrap wood, wiping off excess glue with a fine spatula and wet cloth (Fig. 23.26).

31 When dry, trim the end grain as it shows through the back panels. Clean up the entire chair with abrasive paper, finally softening the edges with Lubrasil paper. You may wish to plug the screw holes.

32 Apply a finish. I used a matt poly-urethane for the pine chair I made, which would also suit ash if you are using that wood. For elm, use linseed oil; oak also looks nice oiled. Personally I avoid using waxes because I find they attract dirt and make subsequent cleaning difficult, but I expect many readers will disagree with me! The thing about wood finishing is that in truth it is an art in itself and very much a matter of personal preferences. If you like the smell of wax and the feeling of 'real wood' etc. etc., and you want the wood to 'breathe', then there are plenty of finishes on the market to choose from. I am not an expert on finishing as such; I use the methods which work for me. Contrary to popular opinion, I find a matt polyurethane varnish not only tough (more so than cell-ulose lacquer), but also easy to apply (a longer working time) and easy to service (you can use warm soapy water to clean your furniture).

Fig. 23.22. The Hitachi jigsaw can be used to remove the bulk of the wood (opposite, above).

Fig. 23.23. Screw on the back pieces (centre, opposite).

Fig. 23.24. Aligning the back pieces (opposite, below).

Fig. 23.25. Routing in the finger grooves.

Fig. 23.26. Tap home the reinforcing strips.

THE JKB COPY CARVING JIG ★★★

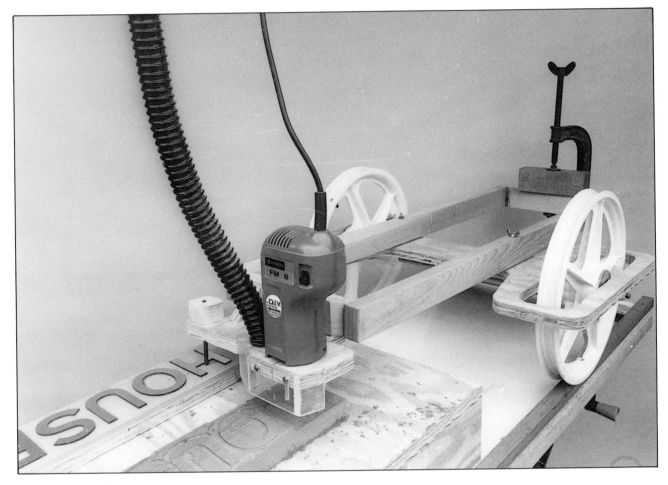

Fig. 24.1. The JKB copy carving jig.

This has to be the ultimate routing jig – a device for **copying in three dimensions!** The potential of the idea is enormous, but before I proceed I should mention that the jig on these pages is a prototype which I designed to test the principle of three-dimensional routing, and that although it works fairly well, ideally it should be made out of steel rather than wood because rigidity is crucial for accuracy. However, the jig is quite suitable for shallow relief copy carving and producing house signs etc. – in other words, fairly light duty work – and it is also quick to make and costs little to build (the wheels are the most expensive part).

The concept was inspired by an American duplicating machine which I saw briefly on video. This machine is made of steel and its moving parts follow a slightly different principle which, although I consider it better, could not be achieved satisfactorily in wood (Fig. 24.2).

The idea is straightforward – copying on a 1:1 ratio, a stylus is mounted at a fixed distance from the router, its profile being exactly the same as the router cutter. Therefore if you change the cutter profile you insert an identical profile stylus (Fig. 24.3). A system of pivoting members allows the stylus and router to move *freely* in three directions – length, width and height. Hence if the stylus traces around a sign or contoured shape, the router will simply duplicate the movement and cut identically into a wood blank. You can make up your own nameplate templates (see House Sign project) using large plastic letters, or use a stencil outfit from any stationers.

With rigidity uppermost in my mind (not rigid thinking!) my first idea was to run four wooden wheels along a twin track, but the need for bearings soon became apparent so the use of 14" nylon bicycle wheels with ball races sprang to mind, and luckily I managed to obtain a pair from a local bicycle shop.

I experimented with wire wrapped around the wheels and anchored at each end of the track (like a draughting board), but the carriage still rocked so I decided to try out a pivoting 'sledge runner' system behind the wheels, and it worked.

Another problem was the horizontal parallelogram action of the arms – how to keep the action rigid without the weight of the router making that end droop. The answer (inspired by a woodworking acquaintance) was to use hinges with their pivot axes running vertically (Fig. 24.4).

The prototype was built in a few hours and therefore was largely based on guess-work, but with a few little extras thrown in at the same time – such as a clear acrylic safety-guard around the cutter and a dust extraction outlet – the jig finally set to work on producing the House Sign project (Fig. 24.5).

Incidentally, in operating the jig for the first time and finding one was naturally holding or steadying it with both hands, I realised how dangerously near my right hand was to the unprotected cutter when guiding the small router head, so a guard is *essential*.

The router I used was the Hitachi FM8 (550 watts) which was absolutely ideal, and is I believe the cheapest router on the current market); the 43mm opening will of course take other routers such as the Bosch POF 500 and the jig can be custom built to take virtually any router. Obviously the plunging facility is not needed. A much larger and sturdier jig (preferably made of steel) could take the Elu 2000 watt router motor, men-

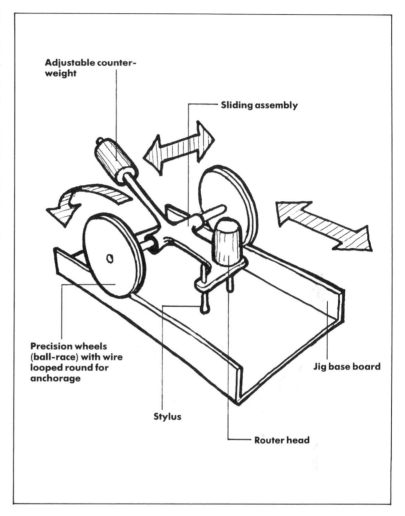

Fig. 24.2. A USA copy carving jig using a pivot rather than a parallelogram principle.

Fig. 24.3. The cutter profile and stylus must be identical.

Fig. 24.4. The pivot axes of the hinges run vertically.

Fig. 24.5. The jig at work on the House Sign project.

tioned in Chapter 5 on Accessories.

The copy carving jig is made of 18mm plywood and solid ash. It is fairly small and readers may wish to completely change the measurements so as to accommodate larger work. Just bear in mind that if it is to be built larger, then it must be beefier.

This jig adequately provides a basis for proportional enlargement. The important thing is that the principle works, and that it will give you endless fun to use and ample room for refinement, if you so wish. If you have access to metalworking facilities, then I would certainly recommend building the jig from angle iron etc.

When using wood, it is preferable to use ash, oak or beech for the swinging arms. Any small bicycle wheel will suffice; the nylon type track perfectly on the inside of the rim. If you use steel wheels which have spoke ends interrupting the inner rim, you can rout a twin groove for tracking (Fig. 24.6). You are likely to purchase the wheels

in a set of front and rear, the rear spindle being stouter, but that is no problem for this jig.

I bedded the wheels into the plywood frame by using Plastic Padding after routing out channels for each spindle. Alignment must be perfect, which can be easily assisted with jigs and tri-squares etc. The jig is so simple that it is best demonstrated by way of illustration (Fig. 24.7).

The building should be more or less self-explanatory, and it is best to work on the separate components in turn but to purchase the bicycle wheels first and decide on your size requirement. Sturdy hinges should be used and carefully selected, as I know they do vary in precision and quality. *There must be absolutely no looseness on the pivoting action.* Perhaps cast brass hinges would suffice. Any plywood or MDF sheet material is suitable for the base board and profiled parts, with a minimum thickness of 18mm. The most stout plywood is

Fig. 24.6. Plan showing the main components of the JKB copy carving jig (opposite, above).

Fig. 24.7. The jig data (opposite, below).

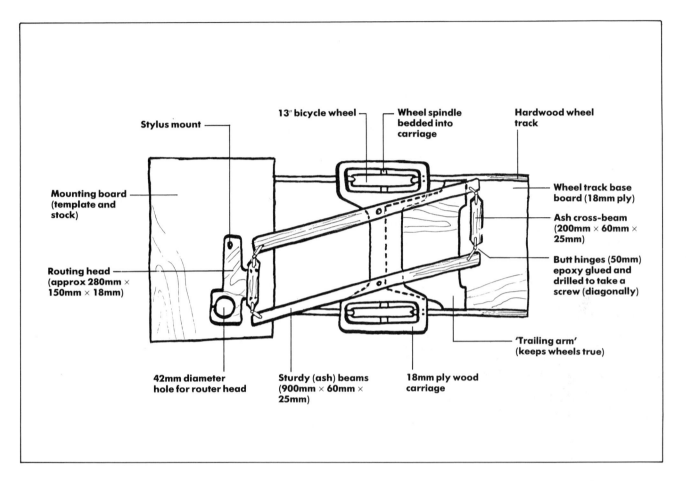

Stylus mount

13″ bicycle wheel

Wheel spindle bedded into carriage

Hardwood wheel track

Mounting board (template and stock)

Wheel track base board (18mm ply)

Ash cross-beam (200mm × 60mm × 25mm)

Routing head (approx 280mm × 150mm × 18mm)

Butt hinges (50mm) epoxy glued and drilled to take a screw (diagonally)

42mm diameter hole for router head

Sturdy (ash) beams (900mm × 60mm × 25mm)

18mm ply wood carriage

'Trailing arm' (keeps wheels true)

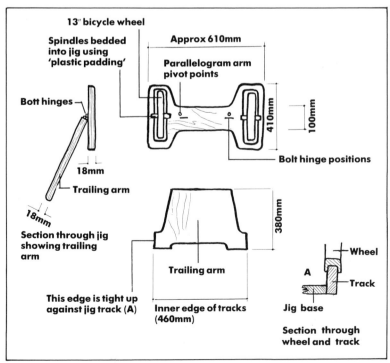

13″ bicycle wheel

Spindles bedded into jig using 'plastic padding'

Approx 610mm

Parallelogram arm pivot points

410mm

100mm

Bott hinges

18mm

Trailing arm

18mm

Bolt hinge positions

Section through jig showing trailing arm

380mm

Trailing arm

Wheel

A

Track

This edge is tight up against jig track (A)

Inner edge of tracks (460mm)

Jig base

Section through wheel and track

beech, but birch will do. Use Cascamite or PVA and screws for reinforcement.

The stylus for this jig is a 6.3mm twist drill inserted upside down with a reinforcing block on top. It corresponds to a $\frac{1}{4}$″ diameter straight cutter. Different profiled styli can be made from any close-grained hardwood and screwed into the head block. I turned up a curved one on the lathe (Fig. 24.3).

The copy carving jig is mounted on the Workmate, but can be bench-mounted on any firm flat surface. The mounting box for the template and stock can be made to adjust vertically if desired, and can also incorporate vacuum clamping. I used the glue gun and also double-sided tape for holding work down (see House Sign project).

This truly creative jig will open up endless routing possibilities for you.

HOUSE SIGN ★★★

Fig. 25.1. A 'House' sign'!

Whether your home has a name or number, or you simply wish to inscribe letters or numbers on to a block of wood for a multitude of purposes, this project complements the project for the JKB Copy Carving Jig and therefore you need to make the jig. Once you have built the inexpensive three-dimensional router copying jig, you can easily and quickly make an accurately inscribed sign.

The template used is purpose built and utilises inexpensive 75mm stick-on plastic letters (widely available from shops specialising in sign materials). Being about 3mm thick, these are ideal for copying round, and of course the finished wooden copy can be routed deeper than 3mm if required.

Once the template is made and secured in the correct position on the mounting table, the appropriate straight cutter and identical profile is set up in the router and router mounting head.

A house sign made of timbers such as figured oak or elm is constructed as follows:

1 Select appropriate plastic letters and carefully glue them on to a plywood or MDF baseboard (Fig 25.2), first marking out the spacings – I used Evostik impact glue. My letters were 75mm high, with spacings of 10mm between them, allowing a 6.3mm diameter cutter to pass freely around the letters.

2 Set up a 6.3mm straight-edged cutter in the router and insert an identical stylus in the stylus holder (I used a 6.3mm twist drill).
3 Carefully mount the template block and wood blank on top of the jig mounting table. First line up the router head with the two blocks positioned correctly width-wise; then check that the blocks lie perpendicular to the router head axis and parallel to each other. (I somehow managed to achieve *italics* the first time I tried out the jig – you may wish to exploit this feature!)

Once the positions of the blocks have been worked out, ensuring that the cutter will cover all the wood in its complete journey, trace positioning marks, then glue-gun down both template block and wood blank. Alternatively, use plenty of double-sided tape.
4 Now position the stylus and cutter on to their respective mounts and adjust the depth of cut by driving the stylus in or out of its holder with a soft mallet. Set the depth of cut to about 2mm. It is crucial when using this wooden jig to make light passes. If you cut much deeper than this, you may get some 'play' in the jig. Repeat cuts can be made to acquire a depth.
5 Start routing and steady both stylus and router with each hand, ensuring your fingers are well away from the cutter (see Fig. 24.5).

I find the most comfortable position is to sit down on a chair so that my head is more

Fig. 25.2. Glue the appropriate letters on to the baseboard. I had to improvise with the 'E'.

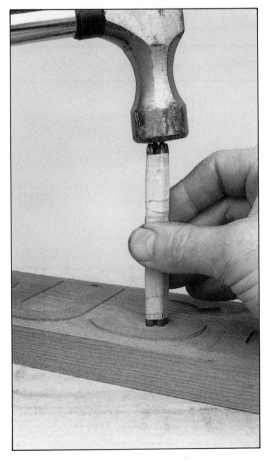

Fig. 25.3. Dressing the surface.

or less level with the action. This really demands the addition of a clear acrylic chippings guard on your jig.

6 Repeat the action until you are happy with the finish and have achieved the desired depth of cut. Now, I should say that it is difficult to achieve a perfect surface finish using the jig. But bear in mind that any fractional (microns) variation of bottom cuts will show as slight circular marks; you even get this if using a router normally on a depth plunge when you are bottoming out a large area. I would imagine that even a steel jig will not give a perfect surface finish and that subsequent cleaning up will be necessary. However, the important thing is that the profile of the letters is crisp and as accurate as the template.

7 Surface 'dress' the house sign, using a bunch of 50mm nails with their heads cut off and ground flat, then wrapped in masking tape and stippled on to the surface using a light hammer (Fig. 25.3).

8 Clean up all edges with fine abrasive paper and apply a suitable finish (polyurethane varnish, or linseed oil).

171

ROLL-TOP WRITING DESK ★★★

Fig. 26.1. Roll-top writing desk.

risks; routing out a fragile panel to all but a millimetre of its thickness and hoping it will bend around a fairly tight track is some risk – but one that was worth taking.

This project was designed in the workshop as I went along, without any calculated drawings other than the measurements of the objects to be accommodated (typewriter/computer etc). I was armed with a sheet of 25mm birch plywood and a tape measure (Fig. 26.2) and I relied on intuition and the versatility of the router to pull me through. This tends to be my style of working. Ideas evolve organically from very basic concepts.

Getting everything right on the drawing board first is far too difficult, but sadly it is the way furniture design is taught in many of our colleges and it simply leads to clinical and 'flat' solutions. Take a chair, for instance. Its most interesting and informative elevation is its side profile and from that elevation you work out (in theory) the ergonomic requirements. But a chair exists in three dimensions and you can only effectively work out those proportions by building a full-size mock-up which you can walk around and experience in all those dimensions. Well, either the visuals count or they don't!

Hopefully, by the time you have worked through some of these projects and mastered the fundamental ABC of routing, you will begin to acquire the confidence to experiment for yourself and become involved in designing the things you wish to make.

I firmly believe that if you learn the essential materials-handling techniques in a creative way in the first place, you will be able to *apply* them creatively. Nevertheless you still need to learn the basic vocabulary. If you learn the techniques in a rigid way then they are always likely to be practised in a limited context. Here endeth the lesson for this project.

This project is perhaps the grand piece of the book, which is not just because of its size, but mainly because the router is put to a fairly stiff challenge: how can you make a **'tambour' roll top** from a single panel of MDF instead of the conventional numerous intricately moulded separate pieces, and achieve the action as well as the looks? The answer is that you can, but not without difficulty! At this point I think it is worth mentioning that if you are in the business of design (a word much bandied about nowadays) you have to be prepared to take

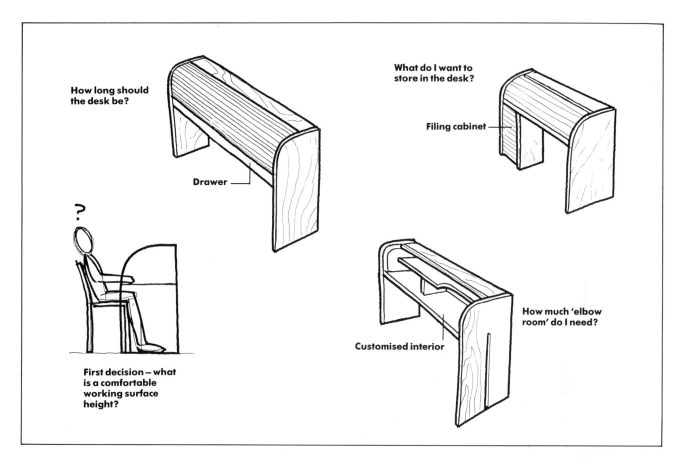

How long should
the desk be?

What do I want to
store in the desk?

Filing cabinet

Drawer

?

Customised interior

How much 'elbow
room' do I need?

First decision – what
is a comfortable
working surface
height?

Yet again the router proved itself master. I cannot imagine any other tool which could have tackled the problem of achieving a roll top by departing from the traditional method. The technology is pushed to its limits in so far as the roll top is routed through to all but one millimetre of its thickness in order to become pliable. The real problem is not so much with the router, but more with the craftsman (or woman), because not only do you need excellent eyesight and a steady hand to operate the router to such fine tolerances, but the material has to be handled with great delicacy while working it. Once the roll-top panel is inserted into its groove, it is home and dry and well supported.

A writing-desk is a highly prized and personal possession. I decided to make this one for myself and to accommodate a particular electric typewriter I have, also A4 paper and two sizes of envelopes. You can

Fig. 26.3. The various design options for the roll-top desk.

Fig. 26.2. The author armed with a tape measure.

Fig. 26.4. The dimensions of the basic carcass.

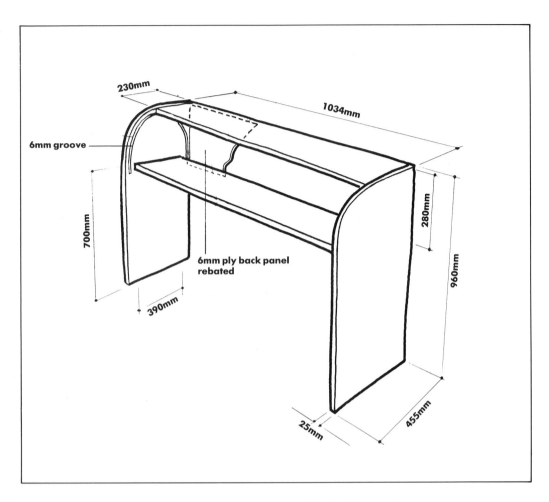

6mm groove

6mm ply back panel rebated

230mm

1034mm

700mm

280mm

960mm

390mm

25mm

455mm

Fig. 26.5. Scribing the curve.

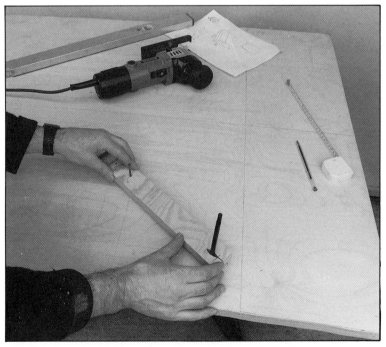

modify the basic design to suit your own needs. I made my desk long enough to accommodate an Amstrad portable computer (PPC512) with a printer (LQ3500) next to it, but changed my mind about the use half-way through! However, it is large enough to accommodate this hardware.

The finish is grey and green: grey-stained birch plywood (highlighting the figure), with a lime green lacquered roll top. But of course you can choose your own colours. Instead of wood stains I used a Dylon fabric dye (Ebony) mixed in hot water and diluted. The exact finish takes some experimenting with, since you have to wipe it off as you put it on. Generally I find water-based stains both deeper-penetrating and easier to apply, and fabric dyes offer a superb range of colours which you can dilute to suit. But more about that later.

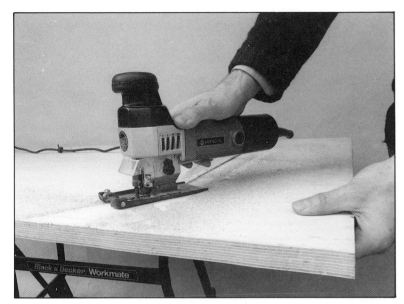

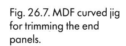

The desk can be 'customised' to suit your particular needs and you may wish to include storage below the table surface (Fig. 26.3). So altogether it is a fairly open-ended design, and it hardly needs mentioning that the router was used to cut the joints!

The stages for making the writing desk are as follows:

1 Select a well-figured and plug-free sheet of 25mm birch plywood (8 × 4) and check that it is not warped.

2 Cut the board into main panels oversize (Fig. 26.4), using a jigsaw with fine blade to minimise grain rip-out.

3 Mark out both end pieces on the appropriate panel, leaving a 3mm gap between for sawing. Scribe the curve using a shop-made trammel (Fig. 26.5).

4 Cut the end pieces with the jigsaw, working slightly outside the marked lines as the router will be used for trimming profiles (Fig. 26.6).

5 Make an MDF jig for router-trimming the curved profile and set up the router with a 12.7mm straight cutter (Fig. 26.7).

6 Carefully trim the ply edge using the router against the MDF template G-clamped in position. Use an 18mm guide bush. Trim the curve, but do not go too far

Fig 26.6. Cut the end pieces with a Hitachi jigsaw.

Fig. 26.7. MDF curved jig for trimming the end panels.

down the front edge as this can be trimmed against a batten.

7 Trim all edges with the batten, carefully clamping it in the correct position (Fig. 26.8). Repeat these operations on the other end piece.

8 Re-work the MDF template, making it smaller to rout the groove for the roll-top panel (Fig. 26.4).

9 Rout a 6.3mm diameter groove around the curved template for the roll-top track. Make sure the cutter does not wander, as this will show. The depth of the groove should be 6mm, and it should start flush with the bottom of the table-top panel at the front and finish 50mm or so below the panel at the rear (Fig. 26.4).

10 Extend the groove at the rear beyond the approximate 50mm mark and rout all the way down the rear of the end pieces, carefully lining up the cutter by attaching a fence (Fig. 26.9). Thoroughly clean up the groove with abrasive paper afterwards to remove any burrs, as a smooth track for the roll top is essential. (The roll top is inserted from the rear along the groove from the base.)

11 Prepare to size the cross panels for the narrow top and the table surface, using the router against a batten to trim the edges.

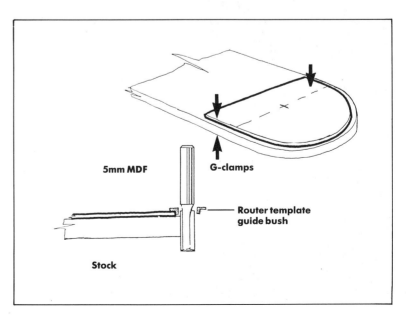

5mm MDF

G-clamps

Router template
guide bush

Stock

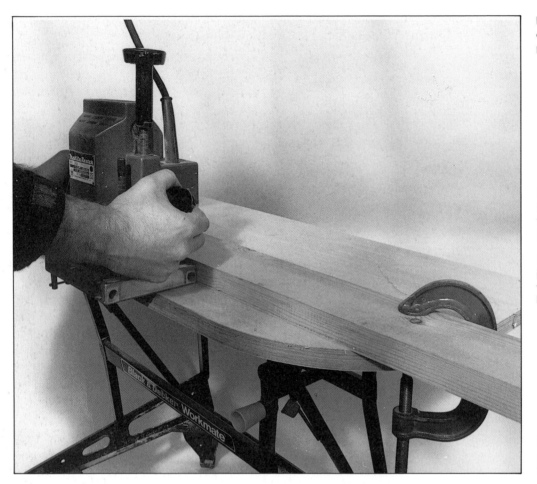

Fig. 26.8. The batten clamped in the correct position.

Fig. 26.10. Rout out the joints for the housings on the cross member ends (opposite, above).

Fig. 26.11. Rout out the joints for the housings on the end pieces (opposite, below).

Fig. 26.9. Routing the groove for the roll-top track.

The overall length should include the housing joints (Fig. 26.4).

12 Set up the router with a 12.7mm diameter straight cutter, and using a straight fence and batten respectively, rout out the joints for the carcass housings on the cross member ends and the end pieces (Figs. 26.10, 26.11).

13 Dry assemble the four members of the carcass, using long sash clamps (or two shorter ones joined together), and on the narrow top cross member plot the curve of the track against one end of the cross member. This portion obviously has to be removed to allow the roll top to glide in its track.

14 Remove the panel and (with a straight fence) rout a series of stepped rebates along the underside of the panel to remove the bulk of this concave feature. The panel

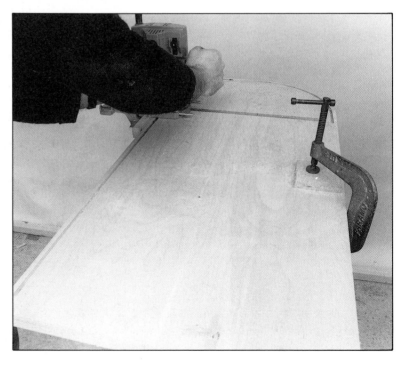

The copy carving jig can
copy in three dimensions.
It produced the 'House'
sign.

The copy carving jig in action on the 'House' sign. The surface is 'dressed' with light stippling.

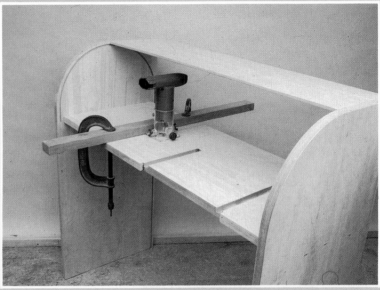

The roll-top desk was the most ambitious project undertaken. The 'tambour' roll top is made from a single panel of MDF!

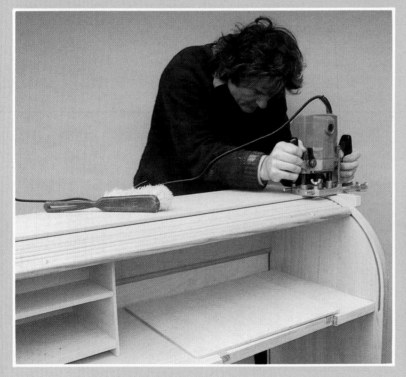

should be recessed slightly further back than the curved line to allow for any slight bowing of the roll top in operation – in other words giving plenty of clearance (Fig. 26.12). When a series of steps has been made with a straight cutter, you can then change to a large radiused cutter and achieve a series of flutings which will eventually make a general concave. Use abrasive paper to finish (Fig. 26.13).

15 Reassemble the four parts of the carcass using sash clamps again and check that everything is square and accurate.

At some point it is advantageous to stick a strip of felt or baize centrally on this concave feature to help soften any contact the roll top might make if it bows. This is really a fine tuning procedure and may not be essential, but is easily inserted after fitting the roll top and testing its glide – and of course it does not show.

Here is where router technology establishes new traditions. The trouble with woodworking is that often it gets entrenched in tradition in a rather stagnant way, but the router is a tool of the late twentieth century and should be used as such.

A common problem in carcass work is the sheer number and complexity of jointed panels which have to be fitted, clamped and glued together square all in one operation. It is a nightmare, only slightly remedied by using a glue which takes all night to go off! Joking apart, the glue-pot life is often the main problem, so why not build the carcass in stages? First build the main carcass members in one operation (e.g. two ends, top and bottom, which in this case we have already completed), glue them together and get them nice and square. Then mark out and rout housings for intermediary panels, sliding them in from the back of course, concentrating on maintaining the squareness. All this is possible using a smaller router, provided you take its height into account when designing.

Well, this is how the desk is built! So, having looked ahead a little in terms of the

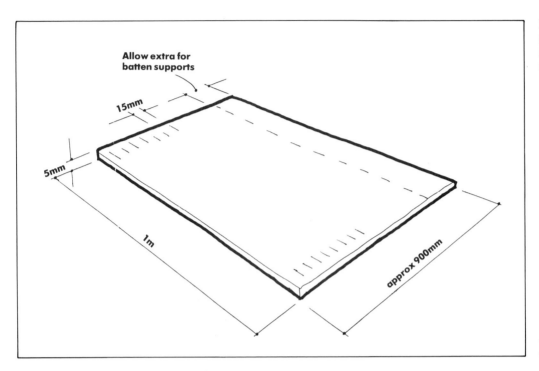

Allow extra for batten supports

15mm

5mm

1m

approx 900mm

Fig. 26.12. Marked positions on the MDF panel for battens for routing grooves.

Fig. 26.13. Make a series of steps with a straight cutter.

construction of your intended design, the basic carcass can now be glued together.

16 Clean up internal carcass surfaces with a power sander (orbital) and abrasive paper hand block, working from medium to fine grades.

17 Set up the carcass in sash clamps for a 'dry' glue run to check everything, then glue and leave overnight, not forgetting to wipe off excess glue with a wet cloth and spatula; bear in mind that the subsequent colour staining will be repelled by glue stains and will stick out like a sore thumb.

18 Now the carcass can be left for the time being while we get to work on the tricky part — the roll top, which has to be routed accurately with numerous parallel grooves. Prepare the 6mm MDF panel exactly 1m long (1000mm) and approximately 900mm wide (its width is trimmed later) and mark out batten positions at 15mm intervals across the width of the panel (Fig. 26.12).

19 Select a dead straight batten and G-clamp it to the MDF panel against a stout plywood backing board ready for routing the grooves in turn. The batten should be positioned exactly on the marks, and I num-

Fig. 26.14. Guide the edge of the router base against the batten.

Fig. 26.15. Groove along the previously routed V-grooves.

bered them identically on each side to avoid any mistake in lining up the batten to unmatching marks. Set up the router with a small V-groove cutter and set to depth *all but two millimetres of the thickness* of the MDF. The board I used was nearer 5mm thick than 6mm, so the crucial thing is the thickness of material you are left with rather than what you start with. (A trial run on scrap MDF really is advisable.)

20 Very carefully, rout in turn each V-groove along the entire length of the panel. I did it in two depth cuts using a Hitachi TR8 router, guiding the edge of its base against the batten (Fig. 26.14). You will see you need the extra width of board to attach the batten on to for the last few grooves. You will find the panel becomes *extremely fragile* and needs very careful handling throughout the entire operation, because the *strength* of it is no longer 5–6mm thick but 2mm thick! Although you can repair it by gluing if you break it, you will probably have a weak spot which shows as a ridge on the working roll top (how could I possibly know that!).

21 Now set up the router with a 4mm diameter straight cutter, *set the depth to all but*

Fig. 26.16. Rout a shallow rebate on the top surface where the panel is buried into the curved groove.

one millimetre of the thickness of the panel and repeat the entire action, *carefully* resetting the battens to the original marks and grooving along the previously routed V-grooves (Fig. 26.15). This now gives a bevelled groove profile which fine tunes the flexibility of the panel by its wide flat bottom

Fig. 26.17. Radiusing the front roll-top strip.

and turns the V-groove into a bevel which visually flows when the roll top is inserted in its curved track. You will notice that the batten guide marks are conveniently located in the middle of the 'slats' and the two stages of routing do not remove them. (Calculating this and the desired flexibility of the roll – i.e. the width of the 'slats' – was the most difficult part of this project for me.)

I would say that this particular routing operation (deceptive though it may look to the reader) is the trickiest you will find in this book, and is immensely satisfying to achieve because of the prolonged concentration required and the fragility of the stock. So don't attempt it after breakfast at the weekend when you are expecting the in-laws for lunch that day! What I am saying is that you need to 'psyche yourself up' to a few hours' concerted effort – and the panel is only safe when it is home and dry in its curved track.

There is one fine adjustment you will need to make – rout a shallow rebate along each

edge on the top surface where the panel is
buried into the curved groove. This is a
tailoring exercise (trial and error), but mark
the width of the rebate at 6mm. This feature
also gives a 'break' between a friction surface (which will wear) and the visible slat
surface which is colour lacquered (and will
show) (Fig. 26.16). A final touch is to rout a
slight bevel along the edge, giving a finished
edge to the 'slats'.

22 Prepare a reinforcing hardwood strip
for the rear end of the roll-top panel (1mm
× 10mm × 6mm) and screw and glue it to
the panel.

23 Prepare the front roll-top strip from suitable hardwood (1mm × 30mm × 20mm)
and rout a groove along it for embedding

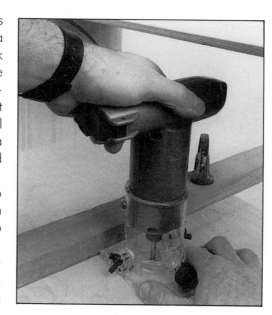

Fig. 26.18. The Makita
cordless trimmer.

Fig. 26.19. Storage space
in the desk.

Fig. 26.20. Various recesses were routed to aid practicality.

Fig. 26. 21. Section through mini-carcass showing location of sliding shelf.

the front edge of the roll top; then radius three edges with a radius cutter – I used a self-guiding cutter set up in a router in the JKB Universal Router table (Fig. 26.17).

24 Rout in appropriate finger grip recesses on to the front roll-top strip, using a large radius cutter and a fence.

25 Clean up strip with abrasive paper.

26 Drill and screw small CSK brass screws through the back of the front strip into the MDF panel, once inserted to secure strip. This enables the strip to be put on after the roll top has been fed into its channel, secured, and taken off if ever needed (such as when repairing the roll top).

27 Insert roll top into its track in the desk and trim where necessary. Screw on front strip, which will serve as a stop for the roll top.

28 Now to return to the fitting out of the internal carcass (which we left at stage 15). The preparation and installation of subsequent carcass panels is a matter of taste

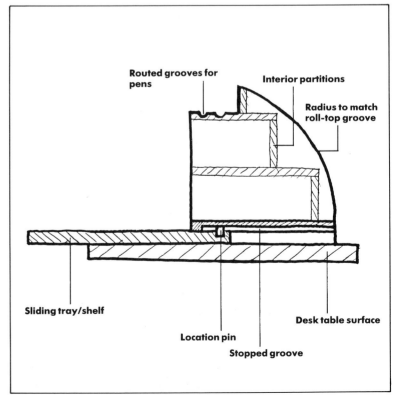

Routed grooves for pens

Interior partitions

Radius to match roll-top groove

Sliding tray/shelf

Location pin

Stopped groove

Desk table surface

Fig. 26.22. Recesses on the table-top front edge allow easy operation of both sliding panels.

and really depends on your particular design, assuming you have on hand a sufficiently small router to follow the method I mentioned earlier (using a smaller router to build the carcass in stages).

I used the Makita cordless trimmer, not because I had a power cut that day but because it is only 190mm high and neatly fits into the confined spaces of the already glued-up carcass (Fig. 26.18). I was also able to use a Hitachi TR8 which is of course beefier, but don't forget that lower-powered routers take a lot longer, and I find the trimmer quite suitable for fairly shallow housings using a maximum 6mm cutter (it is designed for nothing larger than that).

I designed this table to accommodate a Canon S-200 electric typewriter on a sliding tray (dovetail routed track), and it incorporated a mini-carcass for paper and envelopes which was built separately and then routed in, leaving the gluing until last after staining (Fig. 26.19). The construction method for this mini-carcass is butt jointing, which is quite adequate for its size and considering that it is part of a larger carcass when fitted. Make sure you work to a high degree of accuracy. I routed in various recesses for easy removal of paper and envelopes and location of pens on the top (Fig. 26.20). Also there is another sliding tray for paper; it has a single dovetail track and operates against the underneath of the mini carcass to stop it from tilting and coming right out (Fig. 26.21). This panel is fitted when the mini-carcass is glued, which is done after staining. Here again, these are customising details which you may or may not wish to include in your design. Recesses are also included on the table-top front edge for easy operation of both sliding panels (Fig. 26.22).

The typewriter sliding tray is twin dovetail tracked (Fig. 26.23) and includes a groove and round-headed screw stop recessed into the groove flush (Fig. 26.24), which enables

183

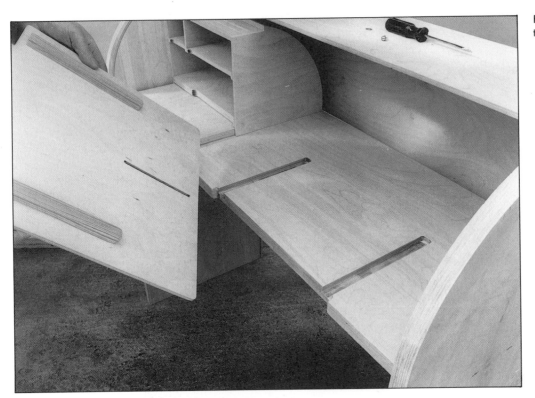

Fig. 26.23. Twin dovetail tracks on the sliding tray.

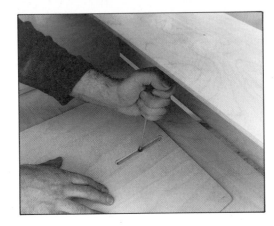

Fig. 26.24. A round-headed screw stop is recessed into the groove flush.

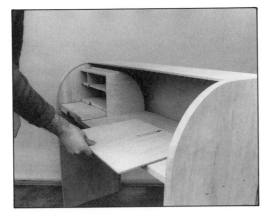

Fig. 26.25. The screw stop prevents the tray from tilting or coming out completely.

the tray to slide out a certain distance without tilting or coming out completely (Fig. 26.25) (the same as the mini carcass sliding tray). Of course, all this is done with the router.

29 Now rout out a small rebate around the back of the desk to take a 6mm plywood back panel (Fig. 26.26). It is simply glued in, after cleaning up in the normal way (Fig. 26.27).

30 A 'Danish shoulder' (see page 67) can be routed into the desk-top where it meets the sides (Fig. 26.28) and cleaned up with abrasive paper.

31 Clean up the entire desk with orbital sander and hand block, using medium to fine grade abrasive paper (Fig. 26.29), and soften all edges slightly (Fig. 26.30) ready for staining and lacquering.

This is the final stage and also a tricky one to do well. Staining is not just a matter of splashing a bit of colour all over the wood and going off to make a cup of tea. The problem is – and particularly in softer woods (no, I didn't say soft woods) – that the stain

Fig. 26.26. A 6mm plywood panel forms the back of the desk.

Fig. 26.27. The back panel is glued in.

Fig. 26.28. A Danish shoulder can be routed in where the desk-top meets the sides.

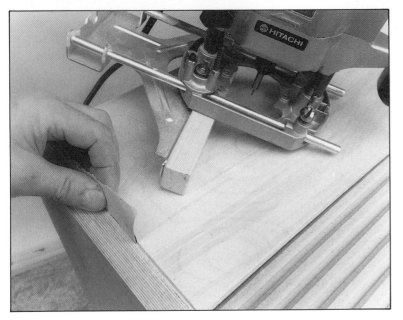

can look dirty where it runs into swirling grain (hard/soft variations in grain texture), and sometimes it is better to mix a stain in with the top coat of a lacquer (i.e. Colron woodstain mixed in with polyurethane varnish), but to apply two clear coats first so that the stain actually 'floats' over the wood and does not penetrate.

Staining is like everything else in that there are preferred methods, but it is not true to say that this particular method works and that one does not – often it's how well it works in a particular situation and how it is applied.

I prefer to use a water-based fabric dye (Dylon, Ebony Black), diluted to give a lovely charcoal grey. You need to try it out on some spare birch plywood first (Fig. 26.31).

Incidentally, many Danes still prefer a bare wood finish, without lacquers, but just a nice soap-and-water build-up protection over the years. It is we in the UK who tend to over-lacquer wood, hence creating a barrier, while at the same time talk about the 'natural touch of real wood'! Finishing is like design, it can easily be overdone. (I have a respect for the simplicity of Scandinavian design.)

35 For this desk I spray-lacquered a few coats of matt cellulose lacquer, first spraying sanding sealer. A matt polyurethane varnish could be brush-applied instead. In either case, very lightly rubbing down between coats with Lubrasil paper keeps the surface smooth.

32 Mask off the glue contact area for the mini-carcass with masking tape as you do not wish to stain this, but gluing it in after staining gives more access to cover the stain on the inside of the desk.

33 Mix up the Dylon stain with hot water. I used an old teapot and transferred it to a Coca Cola bottle. Apply the stain with either a cloth or a brush. As soon as it has been applied, use a dry cloth and wipe it off; then use a wet cloth and wipe it off until all smears have gone and the lovely birch plywood figure glistens through. The actual shade is crucial, and I aim for a kind of medium-density stain effect (Fig. 26.32).

34 Sand down the grain with Lubrasil paper extremely lightly, especially on the edges where the white wood might show through. Water staining raises the grain, but only once, so it is a final smoothing operation. I believe the grain is wetted, raised, then smoothed down in Danish cabinet work (I have seen it done in factories there).

Fig. 26.29. Cleaning up the desk with a Wolf orbital sander.

Fig. 26.31. An unusual stain.

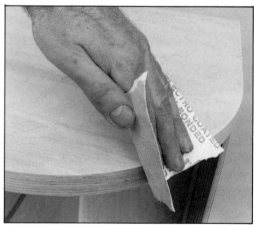

Fig. 26.30. Soften all the edges slightly.

Fig. 26.32. Getting the density right (opposite, above).

Fig. 26.33. Lacquering the roll top (opposite, below).

36 Apply a furniture wax to the dovetailed tracks of the two trays.

37 Remove the masking tape and glue the mini-carcass into position, using clamps. At this stage, insert the sliding tray in its locating tracks.

38 Apply lacquer to the roll top. I used a car-body primer-filler spraycan for the base coat, rubbing down in between with Lubrasil paper. Build up a nice clean finish on the MDF (Fig. 26.33). Apply top cat and spray to choice.

39 When thoroughly cured, insert roll top into desk.

GLOSSARY

Abrasive paper This is a generalised term I use throughout the book, aimed at avoiding the popular but incorrect term 'sandpaper' (which is *not* made of sand). Abrasive papers include GLASSPAPER, the much longer lasting GARNET PAPER, and various industrial abrasive papers such as ALUMINIUM OXIDE PAPER and SILICON CARBIDE PAPER, available in various grits. The finest abrasive papers are FLOUR PAPER, LUBRASIL and 'WET AND DRY' (which is used 'dry').

Arbor The skeleton cutter shank on to which a variety of slotting, slitting and grooving cutters can be fitted, with various spacers and a locking nut.

Ballpoint Worth mentioning because it is a highly effective marking-out tool, superseding the pencil which blunts as it draws.

Batten In routing technology any straight-edged piece of timber used as a guide against which the router passes.

Bevel A simple routed feature where an angled cut is taken off the edge of the wood (also called a chamfer).

Cavetto A quarter-round concave moulding feature.

Collet The chuck of a router which grips specific diameter cutters or reducing sleeves (eg. 6mm, ¼", 9mm etc).

Cove A concave round moulding.

Danish shoulder A narrow gap which runs along the glue or shoulder line of a joint depicting or highlighting the two components. Used mainly on flush surfaces.

Double-sided tape An adhesive tape with substantial bonding capability for holding work down or attaching templates to the work. The more you apply, the better the bond.

Dogs Traditionally, sprung metal inserts for securing the work to the bench. The dogs are placed in spaced mortises in the benchtop and adjusted for height. Plastic dogs are used extensively in the Black & Decker Workmate illustrated throughout this book.

Electronic Referring to the modern generation of routers which have a variable speed motor (8000–25 000 rpm) for easy

start, and speed selection for different diameter cutters (the larger the diameter the slower the speed).

Epoxy Glue or resin. Extremely strong adhesive used in the boatbuilding industry but also of particular advantage for external woodworking. Normally mixed with a catalyst (hardener).

Fence A straight-edged guide to a router (a wheel fence is an attachment for curved work). Fence routing is commonly used for rebating, edge profiling and grooving.

Fixed head routing. Either overhead or inverted where the router motor or head is anchored to the table, as opposed to hand held routing.

Flute Generally refers to the cutting edge of cutters (single or twin flute). Twin flute are more efficient but not available in diameters under 3mm. 'Fluted' refers to a profiled section, usually a series of parallel concave cuts on a board.

Glue gun A hot-melt glue method. Instant bonding, ideal for temporary bonds, i.e. fixing work to bench etc.

HSS High speed steel. High carbon content steel used for cutters.

Incredible That cannot be believed, hard to believe, surprising.

Jig A generalised term for a device which attaches to the router, the work or both, and acts as a holding and guiding mechanism.

Laminating A confusing term. In woodworking the bonding together of thin strips of wood (usually bent) in a former to achieve a thicker and hence stronger laminate.

Leading edge A woodworking term applied to the way a chisel is offered into the wood to start a cut.

Linisher A belt sanding machine for flat and concave sanding.

Masking tape A stretchy tape with excellent bonding qualities which can be used extensively as a clamping method.

MDF Medium Density Fibreboard. A characterless material with immense versatility in the woodworking industry. It is smoother than hardboard and denser than chipboard, allowing edge profiling and finishing. Avail-

able in large boards from 6mm thickness upwards.

Mounting lug A small block of wood, hot-melt bonded to the work so as to allow it to be held in the vice and raised for router cutter clearance if needed. It is a temporary structure.

Pass In routing technology it means one straight-through stroke of the router into the work!

Plunge The lowering of the router cutter into the work achieved by most modern routers.

Polyester Resin Similar to epoxy resin, it is the 'P' in GRP and comes in liquid form (petrochemical). When a hardener is added to it it becomes like glass.

PVA Polyvinyl acetate glue. The most popular modern adhesive. Trade name 'Evostik Resin W'. It dries under pressure in about two hours at 60° Fahrenheit. Not a good gap filler. Relies on excellent surface-to-surface contact (tight joints).

Rate of feed The speed at which a pass is made – the speed at which the cutter journeys across the wood.

Rout Force or fetch out.

Short grain Where the length of fibres is less than the width of the cut, resulting in a weak structure. An example is in a mortise and tenon 'L' connection. The wood between the mortise and the end of the component has 'short grain' and in the normal leverage of this shape of joint, would easily break.

Shuttering plywood Used extensively in the construction industry, in various grades, the only one suitable here is 'good one side' specification.

Stock The work or specific piece of timber or other material being worked.

Square Equal sided (as in square-sectioned material) or a loose term meaning −90 degrees in practical work, used in connection with a tri-square which has a 90-degree blade.

TCT Tungsten carbide tipped – usually referring to saw blades and router-cutter bits. Much harder-wearing and longer-lasting than HSS.

SUPPLIERS

Bicycle Wheels
Bath Cycle Centre,
Unit 1, Chelsea House,
London Road,
Bath.

Clock Movements
Southern Watch & Clock Supplies Ltd,
Precista House,
48 High Street, Orpington,
Kent.

Toolmail,
170 High Street,
Lewes,
East Sussex BN7 1YU.

Cutters
Trend Machinery & Tools Ltd,
Unit N,
Penfold Works,
Imperial Way,
Watford,
Herts.

Epoxy Glue
SP Systems,
Cowes,
Isle of Wight.

The Incredible Router
Video Thinking Hand Video,
PO Box 658,
Bath BA1 6ED.

Leigh Dovetail Jig
SMS Woodworking Machinery,
Danesford,
Pamber Road, Silchester,
Near Reading.

Medium Density Fibreboard (MDF)
Caberboard Ltd,
Cowie,
Stirlingshire.

Wolfcraft UK
Zebra Tool Co.,
Unit 24,
South Hampshire Ind. Park,
Totton,
Southampton.

Zyliss Clamp
Westminster Trading Co.,
72 Albert Street,
London NW1 7NR.

Fibre collet sleeves, cutters
Method Tools Ltd,
Disley
Cheshire
SK12 2NN.

INDEX

OTHER TITLES AVAILABLE FROM GMC PUBLICATIONS LTD:
Woodworking Plans and Projects
40 More Woodworking Plans and Projects
Woodworking Crafts Annual
Sharpening and Care of Woodworking Tools and Equipment   John Sainsbury
Turning Miniatures in Wood   John Sainsbury
Woodcarving: A Complete Course   Ron Butterfield
Pleasure and Profit from Woodturning   Reg Sherwin
Creating a Miniature World   Patricia King
Making Unusual Miniatures   Graham Spalding
Furniture Projects for the Home   Ernest Parrott
Seat Weaving   Ricky Holdstock
Green Woodwork   Mike Abbott
Care and Repair   5th edition of the essential handbook
Directory of Members of the Guild of Master Craftsmen 1989–90

All these books may be ordered by post from the publishers at 166 High Street, Lewes, East Sussex BN7 1XU, telephone (0273) 477374. Please write or phone for further details. Credit card orders are accepted.